IT'S A CONSPIRACY!

**The world's wildest conspiracy theories.
What *they* don't want you to know.
And why the truth is out there.**

Also by Tom Cutler

The First Da Capo Songbook (as Fred Plowright)

The Second Da Capo Songbook (as Fred Plowright)

Speak Well English: an guide for aliens to successful intercourse in the correctly English mode (as Tomas Santos)

211 Things a Bright Boy Can Do

211 Things a Bright Girl Can Do (as Bunty Cutler)

A Gentleman's Bedside Book: entertainment for the last fifteen minutes of the day

Found in Translation: a extremely guide to speak correctly English (as Tomas Santos)

The Gentleman's Instant Genius Guide: become an expert in everything

Slap and Tickle: the unusual history of sex and the people who have it

The Pilot Who Wore a Dress: and other dastardly lateral thinking mysteries

Keep Clear: my adventures with Asperger's

TOM CUTLER

IT'S A CONSPIRACY!

HarperCollins*Publishers*

HarperCollins*Publishers*
1 London Bridge Street
London SE1 9GF

www.harpercollins.co.uk

HarperCollins*Publishers*
1st Floor, Watermarque Building, Ringsend Road
Dublin 4, Ireland

First published by HarperCollins*Publishers* 2021

1 3 5 7 9 10 8 6 4 2

© Tom Cutler 2021

MIX
Paper from
responsible sources
FSC™ C007454

This book is produced from independently certified FSC™ paper
to ensure responsible forest management.

For more information visit: www.harpercollins.co.uk/green

To the memory of
William of Ockham

People almost invariably arrive at their beliefs not on the basis of proof but on the basis of what they find attractive.

—BLAISE PASCAL

Contents

IV LIGHTING THE FUSE
Historical Conspiracies

V ON THE WARPATH
Military Conspiracies

VI UNDER THE MICROSCOPE
Science and Health Conspiracies

VII BIG BROTHER IS WATCHING YOU
Inside Jobs and Government Dirty Tricks

VIII WHO'S PULLING THE STRINGS?
Secret Societies That Run the World

IX THE X FILES
The Weirdest of All Conspiracies

Introduction

Just because you're paranoid doesn't
mean they're not out to get you.

—ANON

We all love a good conspiracy theory, don't we! In this
age of science, and more than three hundred years since
the Enlightenment, polls show that half of American
adults believe at least one conspiracy theory, while more
than three-quarters believe in angels. A conspiracy theory
is not only the belief that one person is conspiring with
another, it also takes in the idea that some shadowy and
powerful organisation is involved in skulduggery that is
harming ordinary people. I believe all conspiracy theories
– except the ones that aren't true. And there's the problem: sorting the true from the false.

In the fourteenth century, a Franciscan friar named
William of Ockham (or Occam) popularised a nifty rule,
now known as 'Occam's razor', which he said was useful
when you were trying to find out what was true. His idea
was that, in general, the simplest of competing theories is
probably the right one. Five hundred years later Occam's

razor is still handy – *though not always*. Sometimes, just to confuse everybody, the correct answer is the more elaborate one – as with, say, the Watergate conspiracy (*see page 165*).

So, what is it that drives all of us a bit, and some of us a lot, to accept these ideas? In normal life we tend to believe things based on the evidence. If a friend tells us it's raining, we will probably look out of the window to check for ourselves. But if she says she's heard that the Moon landings were faked, or that vaccines are dangerous, we are more likely to take her word for it.

We seem to be naturally amenable to these stories, and today, beset as we are by rapid change, worrying complexity, global disease threats and troubling concerns about the quality and competence of our political leaders, conspiracy theories make a brilliant labour-saving tool.

Viren Swami, professor of social psychology at Anglia Ruskin University, says that conspiratorial thinking surges during such periods of societal crisis, when, yearning for meaning and control in their lives, people tend to believe that dark forces are shaping events in an endless battle between good and evil.

For many, politics is no longer a matter of Right and Left; instead it's Us against Them. This leads authoritarian right-wingers to cuddle up with probiotic lefties in claims that an apocalyptic 'Brave New World Order' is coming or that Paul McCartney is a clone. So many people have fallen down conspiracy-theory rabbit holes that the BBC now employs a 'specialist disinformation reporter'.

INTRODUCTION

Believing that the Earth is hollow or that Paul McCartney died years ago is pretty harmless. The trouble starts when conspiracy theories go from harmless fun to funless harm. The online movement QAnon, which sprang out of the notorious 'Pizzagate' conspiracy theory in 2016 (*see page 210*), has been characterised as a threat by social media platforms and the FBI. Its basic claim when it began was that President Donald Trump was fighting a secret war against a 'deep state' cabal of satanic paedophiles that included Democrats, billionaires and Hollywood celebrities. The superspreading of such patently fishy conspiracy theories by and among QAnon's apostles has nonetheless given these followers a profound sense of purpose, power and belonging.

In the end, of course, all conspiracy theories are intriguing, and the best compelling, which may be why so many have lasted so long. Like the old wives' tales of yesteryear, some are very probably true, others only possibly true, and a final few have turned out to be pure moonshine, though no less enjoyable for that.

In this book I take a meander through a variety of the most beguiling, from the UK, Europe and the USA – a country offering a seam especially rich in conspiracy gold. There's a conspiracy theory here for every taste, and what better diversion from the grim reality of the twenty-four-hour news cycle than jumping into a world run by a secret society of Lizard Men from outer space, where Finland is fake and Elvis is still with us, running his rhinestone flares through the rinse cycle down at the Memphis laundromat?

Some of these conspiracy theories, and *theorists*, will make you laugh, others will make you think, and with at least one 'Hey, Martha!' moment per page, showcasing some especially curious and sparkling nugget, you'll find yourself frequently elbowing your partner in the ribs.

But, before you begin, here's a bit of advice. Try to dodge the temptation to start in the foothills of page one and then hike non-stop to the very top of the mountain, as you would with *Madame Bovary*. Instead, treat this more like a sauna: nip in quick somewhere, thrash yourself with a few twigs and get out sharpish for a splash in the cold pond. Later you can have another go, on a different page. By taking it in short bursts, I hope you will be able to detach yourself pleasantly from the cares of the world without getting all hot and bothered.

Anyway, without further ado, it is now time to put on your tinfoil hat, take a deep lungful of air and launch yourself boldly out into the wild unknown of Conspiracyland ...

I

DEATH BY DESIGN

Assassination Conspiracies

A wise man proportions his
belief to the evidence.

—DAVID HUME

Death of a Princess

Shortly after midnight on the morning of 31 August 1997, thirty-six-year-old Diana, Princess of Wales, and her suitor Dodi Fayed were about to leave the Ritz Hotel in Paris to travel to a nearby flat – both properties owned by Dodi's fantastically rich father. Outside the building on Place Vendôme, thirty or so paparazzi were waiting, itching to get a snap of the glamorous couple. In an effort to dodge these charming gentlemen, a cunning plan had been devised. A decoy vehicle would be standing by, which, on a signal, would leave the Ritz from the main entrance. Diana and Dodi would then quietly depart from the hotel's back door to be driven to their flat in a black Mercedes-Benz by the Ritz's deputy head of security, Henri Paul.

The couple's car left the hotel as planned and sped through the Paris streets, pursued on motorbikes by the hardened paparazzi, who had greeted the decoy vehicle with loud cries of 'We weren't born yesterday!'

A little before 12.30 a.m. the Mercedes entered the dark Pont de l'Alma tunnel, going at about 65 mph, more than twice the speed allowed in this Paris underpass. Here, Paul lost control of the car and smashed into a pillar, bouncing off and crashing backwards into the tunnel wall.

Emergency vehicles were quickly on the scene, where Fayed and Paul were both pronounced dead. Diana was still just able to speak but had received catastrophic injuries to her heart. She was taken to hospital, where she died shortly afterwards. She was quickly embalmed, ruling out a proper post-mortem. Also in the car was bodyguard Trevor Rees-Jones, who had been seriously injured: his face crushed flat. He was the only member of the party to survive. The dead occupants had not been wearing seat belts.

In the investigations that followed, Paul, who had drunk about five measures of Ricard, an anise-flavoured spirit, was declared solely responsible for the crash. The British inquest reached a verdict of unlawful killing through grossly negligent driving.

But it was not long before questions were being asked about what had actually been going on that night, and a number of conspiracy theories were soon in the air. Suggested conspirators included Iran, the CIA, Islamic militants and the Freemasons, who, it was said, had arranged for the crash to take place under that notorious masonic icon: a stone bridge. Inconveniently for this theory, however, the Pont de l'Alma tunnel is actually made of concrete and tarmac, and the bridge itself is a 1974 cement-and-girder number.

Analysis of the crashed car revealed traces of white paint on its black bodywork. This belonged to a white Fiat Uno and it was suggested that this car had been used to cause the Mercedes to swerve and crash. The Fiat was said to belong to a young taxi driver who was identified by witnesses as the 'agitated man' they believed they had seen at the scene. But in the end, all this speculation met a brick wall.

The real clue, it was claimed, lay in Diana's well-known campaigning against land mines, though in this she was not the only famous campaigner. In fact, nobody in the world has ever campaigned *for* these disgusting weapons, except, of course, international arms makers. The conjecture was that it was they who had arranged the so-called 'accident' to put a stop to the princess's unhelpful speeches on the subject.

The Libyan leader Colonel Gaddafi, 'Brother Leader' of the Great Socialist People's Libyan Arab Jamahiriya, had his own thoughts. He explained that the death of Princess Diana was a joint Franco-British conspiracy to stop the beautiful and headstrong English princess marrying an Arab. But Gaddafi was a noted oddball. BBC World Affairs Editor John Simpson recalled in his 2001 memoir *A Mad World, My Masters* that during one long interview in a hot tent Gaddafi repeatedly broke wind – and with some gusto. He would rise up a little in his chair, said Simpson, 'the thunder would roll for fifteen or twenty seconds at a time, and then he would sink back into his seat with a pleased expression on his face'.

There really was no shortage of suspected conspirators. The trouble was, it couldn't have been all of them. Perhaps, though, she wasn't actually dead …

Had Diana faked her death? The evidence was said to be clear: instead of an open casket like that of Mother Teresa – who died days later – she had 'been buried' in a closed coffin. This was not, perhaps, the most robust idea doing the rounds, and seemed to have come from an American thinker who was unaware that in Britain open coffins are as rare as white peacocks; it's not the British way of doing things, whether the occupant is royal or common.

But maybe Diana was not even the target. Could it have been Dodi – murdered by enemies of his famous father, Mohamed?

At the time of writing Mohamed Al-Fayed is in his nineties, a powerful businessman who made enemies over the years and was denied British nationality after questions came up over his dealings. In a strange irony it was this Anglophile Egyptian himself – who added the decorative 'Al' to his name in the early 1970s – who was responsible for the conspiracy theory that generated more publicity than any other.

Months after the accident, in his usual plainspoken way, Al-Fayed alleged that the crash had been the result of a conspiracy arranged by MI6 under the direction of the Duke of Edinburgh. According to the BBC, former MI6 officer Richard Tomlinson gave support to this musing. Tomlinson apparently asserted that the driver, Henri Paul, was working for the security services. He also said that the tunnel crash mirrored plans he had seen to use a strobe light to blind the chauffeur of a foreign president.

Al-Fayed claimed that former prime minister Tony Blair, MI5, MI6 and the British ambassador to France were all part of the conspiracy, and that Princess Diana 'knew Prince Philip and Prince Charles were trying to get rid of her'. Al-Fayed also alleged that Prince Charles had arranged to have Princess Diana assassinated so he could marry his 'crocodile wife' Camilla Parker Bowles, though evidence for this fancy was unforthcoming. Strangely enough, however, the prince did finally marry Camilla. So, were these speeding paparazzi really press photographers, or were they secret agents trained to ride at speed, possibly a highly expert 'wet team', so-called because they are involved in operations where blood is spilt?

Al-Fayed expanded on his inside-job idea, telling the *Daily Express* that Diana and Dodi had been about to announce their engagement, and that at the time of her death, the princess had been expecting a baby. The hypothesis was then floated that the Royal Family did not want one of their in-law princesses to have a Muslim boyfriend. Neither, it was claimed, did they welcome the notion of the future king of England, and head of the country's Anglican Church, having a Muslim stepfather. Others reckoned it was the idea of having Mohamed Al-Fayed himself round for cucumber sandwiches, more than his family's religion, that raised their gorge. Are somebody's rough-diamond table manners really enough to cause his son's future parents-in-law to arrange with British intelligence organisations to have him bumped off along with their own current daughter-in-law? Who can say?

A Metropolitan Police inquiry named Operation Paget was set up in 2004 to investigate the various conspiracy theories but was wound up after the British inquest in 2008.

The Murder of God's Banker

Sometime around 7.30 in the morning of Friday, 18 June 1982, a postman walking along the embankment of the River Thames in London noticed the body of a man hanging by his neck from some scaffolding under Blackfriars Bridge. The police were called, and when they took him down they found that his pockets had been stuffed with bricks, and one had been pushed into the open fly of his trousers. Along with the bricks, they also discovered an Italian passport and $15,000 in three different currencies.

The cadaver was that of Roberto Calvi, chairman of the large, privately owned Italian bank Banco Ambrosiano, which had just collapsed, with gigantic debts, causing a political scandal. Much of the missing money belonged to the Mafia and a lot of the rest had been deposited by Banco Ambrosiano's main shareholder, the Istituto per le Opere di Religiose (the Institute of Religious Works), effectively the bank of the Holy See, or, in plainer words, the Vatican Bank. For this reason, Roberto Calvi was popularly known as 'God's banker', but quite what he knew of the Mafia money in the Vatican vaults was an interesting question.

The banking failure might well have caused shame in a deeply religious man, enough perhaps to make him do away with himself, but, there again, it all looked a bit funny. First, Signor Calvi had gone missing from his Rome apartment a week earlier, having shaved off his distinctive moustache. He had then flown to London on a false passport in the name of Gian Roberto Calvini. Second, there were some odd things about his 'suicide'. For example, the dusty bricks found in his pockets had left no marks on the victim's fingers. And who unzips his trousers and stuffs a brick in there before saying his prayers and kicking away the ladder? That looked more like an act of post-mortem humiliation by somebody else and it was not long before rumours were circulating that this was not suicide, but a murder conspiracy.

As soon as the word 'conspiracy' was mentioned, people, from habit, turned their attention to the Masons, and this time there was good reason. Calvi had been a member of the exclusive and shady masonic lodge Propaganda Due, or P2, which was run by Italian financier Licio Gelli. Propaganda Due was described as a 'state within a state' and had among its members the heads of the Italian intelligence services, senior military leaders, journalists with clout, parliamentarians and businessmen, including a fellow called Silvio Berlusconi, who became famous for being prime minister of Italy and having purple hair.

When police searched Gelli's villa, they found the 'Plan for Democratic Rebirth', an interesting document calling for consolidation of the media, suppression of trade unions and the rewriting of the Italian Constitution. This sounds like what has been going on for some time in more than one country.

Members of P2 were known as '*frati neri*' or 'black friars', leading some to suggest that Blackfriars Bridge was a significant location for Calvi's murder. On the other hand, the bridge is only three minutes from the Fleet Street branch of McDonald's, but nobody was suggesting that Ronald McDonald had anything to do with it.

Despite the questions no definite answers came to light, which is the mark of an efficient conspiracy. However, in 1991 a Mafia informant claimed that Calvi had indeed been killed, over the regrettable loss of Mafia funds. The killer was, he said, one Francesco Di Carlo, a gentleman resident in London at the time. Di Carlo denied this, though he admitted he had been asked. According to him, the real killers were a couple of cheeky rascals named Vincenzo Casillo and Sergio Vaccari. Neither denied it, both having come over a bit dead.

In 1998, Calvi's body was exhumed and an independent forensic report decided that he had indeed been murdered, his neck injuries being 'inconsistent with hanging'. The report also noted the absence of rust and flaking paint on his shoes, which ought to have come off the scaffolding over which he was supposed to have clambered.

In 2005, Licio Gelli, leader of the Propaganda Due masonic lodge, was investigated on charges of ordering Calvi's murder, along with Calvi's sometime driver and bodyguard, and a bunch of other scamps. The charges: that Calvi was done in to prevent him from blackmailing P2, the Vatican Bank and the Mafia. Gelli acknowledged that Calvi, the man who knew too much, had indeed been done to death, but denied involvement and was not tried. In 2007, the death was ruled a murder in Italy but all the accused were acquitted owing to 'insufficient evidence'. It has since been claimed that senior figures in the Italian Establishment who actually ordered the murder of God's banker most probably escaped prosecution altogether.

The Mysterious Death of Marilyn Monroe

Marilyn Monroe was the most popular and successful Hollywood sex symbol of the fifties and sixties, but, in the early morning of Sunday, 5 August 1962, this glamorous film star was found dead in the blank, impersonal and untidy bedroom of her Los Angeles home. She was just thirty-six years old.

A strange, dislocated character, Marilyn had been self-absorbed, anxiety prone and unsettled for many years. Laurence Olivier described her as a 'divided personality' who could be charming and lovable one minute and seriously frightening the next. She was a dedicated drinker and long-time pill-popper.

Though still young, Monroe was affected by a variety of health troubles and had lost a great deal of weight after recent gallbladder surgery. Yet in screen tests for, and footage from, *Something's Got to Give*, the film she was making at the time of her death, she appears perfectly lucid and is still uncommonly alluring.

On the day in question, Monroe had pushed off to bed at about 8 p.m., where she took a call from a friend, the actor and socialite Peter Lawford, who was also brother-in-law to Attorney General Robert 'Bobby' Kennedy and his brother President John F. Kennedy. She asked Lawford to 'say goodbye to the president and say goodbye to yourself, because you're a nice guy'. He was alarmed by Marilyn's voice and believed she was under the influence of drugs. At his worried urging, Lawford's agent called Monroe's lawyer, who rang the house but was reassured by her housekeeper, Eunice Murray, that there was nothing amiss.

At about three in the morning, Murray noticed light under Monroe's bedroom door, which she tried but, unusually, found locked. She called Marilyn's psychiatrist, Ralph Greenson, who suggested that she look in through a window. Murray did so and saw Monroe under a sheet, lying face down on the bed.

Greenson arrived shortly afterwards and entered the room by breaking a window. He found Monroe dead, with empty pill bottles beside her. He called her doctor, who arrived at around 3.50 a.m., and confirmed her death. Sometime later, at 4.25, they notified the police.

The news soon hit the front pages, the headlines reporting IT LOOKS LIKE SUICIDE. There were no signs of nefarious doings at Monroe's house, and the coroner decided her death had probably been deliberate, based on the large number of powerful sedatives she had taken, her frequent mood swings, previous overdoses and suicidal thinking.

On 8 August the actress's body was interred in a crypt at the sentimentally named Corridor of Memories, and, after the welter of publicity and hand-wringing had died down, suicide was taken to be the last word on her death.

The first suggestions that Monroe might have been murdered came in a self-published 1964 booklet, *The Strange Death of Marilyn Monroe* by Frank A. Capell, an antisemitic, anti-communist activist and writer. Capell suggested that Monroe had been murdered as part of a communist conspiracy, and claimed that the president's brother, Bobby Kennedy, was a communist sympathiser. He further announced that Bobby and Monroe had had an affair and that Bobby had ordered her killing to stop her spilling the beans and causing a scandal. At the time, his relationship with Marilyn was a big secret.

Other conspiracy theorists soon joined the party, but sometimes their contributions only added mystery to the enigma. In 1975, author Robert F. Slatzer said in passing that he had been Monroe's husband for three days in 1952, an announcement that did not take things very much further. Another alleged that Marilyn was murdered by the CIA in revenge for the Bay of Pigs Cuban-invasion fiasco. It remained unclear quite what role Monroe had played in the Bay of Pigs, or what she had done during that unfortunate escapade that required her to be murdered.

Frank Capell's friend, police sergeant Jack Clemmons, claimed he was the first police officer at Monroe's house that night and said he had noticed her housekeeper washing her sheets. She was later allowed, he said, to travel to Europe. This must have been the first time that possible sheet-laundering had been suggested as reason enough to forbid foreign holidays.

The first bit of new information came out in 1976, when journalist Anthony Scaduto alleged under his pen name Tony Sciacca that Marilyn had kept a red diary in which she recorded the political pillow talk she had picked up from the Kennedys. He also claimed that union boss Jimmy Hoffa had arranged for the bugging of Marilyn's house in the hope of collecting material that could be used against the Kennedys, neither of whom was on his Christmas-card list. Nobody could get a comment out of Jimmy, as he had disappeared the previous year after arranging to have a friendly lunch with a couple of his organised-crime chums, whose mug shots give you the willies.

The conspiracy theories bubbled away over the years, until in 1982 a nice man called Lionel Grandison, who had been fired from the coroner's office for stealing from corpses, was quoted as saying that the Monroe autopsy had failed to mention that her body was heavily bruised. He also said the 'red diary' – which nobody had ever seen – had vanished. For obvious reasons, neither of these claims could be investigated.

In 1985, conspiracy-theory expert and serious writer Anthony Summers, author of a sizzling exposé of J. Edgar Hoover and an investigation of Mafia and CIA involvement in the Kennedy assassination (*see page 18*), wrote a book entitled *Goddess: The Secret Lives of Marilyn Monroe*. Summers had interviewed several hundred people and concluded that towards the end of her life Monroe had been a delusional alcoholic and drug addict who had had affairs with both Robert Kennedy and the president. He suggested that when Bobby Kennedy ended their affair, Marilyn threatened to let the cat out of the bag. So, claimed Summers, Kennedy and Peter Lawford kept her in check by feeding her drugs and booze. He said Monroe had been hysterical and had overdosed by accident, dying in the ambulance on the way to hospital. Because Bobby Kennedy wanted to leave town before the death was announced, her body had been taken back to the house, where, with the involvement of Lawford, the Kennedys and J. Edgar Hoover, the accidental overdose was made to look like a suicide. There were, indeed, reports that Robert Kennedy had been spotted near the house on that evening.

Over the years, other well-known authors joined in with their own take on the various conspiracy theories. In 1993, Donald Spoto said there were some intriguing extra details to add. Marilyn had, he explained, taken barbiturates prescribed by her doctor, yet had not told her psychiatrist, who then prescribed her a chloral hydrate enema. It was the deadly dual action of these sedative drugs coming at her, as it were, from both ends that did the damage. To cover up, Marilyn's doctors and housekeeper worked out the suicide story. Other theorists claimed the enema was actually given by Monroe's housekeeper, who was really her nurse. One conspiracy theorist was even accused of making up uncomfortably detailed enema conspiracy theories to satisfy his own sexual fetish.

Poor old Marilyn. With friends like that, who needs enemas?

The Assassination of John F. Kennedy

Of all the conspiracy theories in the world the Kennedy assassination is the richest in story. Indeed, this subject has spawned films and books aplenty and I can only skim the surface.

Shortly before 12.30 p.m. on 22 November 1963, the young and handsome Democrat President John Fitzgerald Kennedy (JFK) was being driven in an open-topped Lincoln Continental limousine through downtown Dallas, at the head of a presidential motorcade. He hoped this trip to the oil-rich South would boost campaign contributions for his anticipated re-election the next year. In the vehicles behind sat dignitaries, security men, press people and other politicians, including the vice president, Lyndon Baines Johnson (LBJ). Smiling bystanders lined the sunny streets, applauding the president's approach. At the same time, a smattering of extreme right-wing Southerners, many of them expatriate anti-Castro Cubans, were cursing Kennedy over his half-hearted support for the CIA-backed Bay of Pigs invasion attempt that had gone horribly wrong in Cuba two years before.

At 12.30 the motorcade turned into Dealey Plaza, an open area surrounded by tall business and civic buildings, a railway yard and parking lots. After taking a viciously sharp left turn, the long car's progress slowed to a crawl, at which moment a fusillade of shots rang out.

Kennedy was hit in the throat, close to his tie knot. In a reflex motion he raised his hands to his neck but was then shot in the back, before another shot blasted his head open, sending an aerosol of blood and brain matter behind him, spattering the motorcycle outrider to his rear left. Visible in photographs afterwards was a man standing on the kerb, close to the car, holding an open black umbrella in the noonday sun. At the moment of the head shot, he lifted the umbrella high above his head and gesticulated with it dramatically. Having braked almost to a stop, the motorcade now accelerated away to a nearby hospital. The umbrella man was not approached or asked what he was doing, although his suspicious movements could be seen from all over the plaza. Years later, during investigations by the United States House of Representatives Select Committee on Assassinations, a man identified as the umbrella man was questioned about his behaviour but reduced the room to helpless laughter by forcing a demonstration umbrella inside-out. That was the end of that.

On top of a hillock behind the umbrella man was a fenced parking lot. A deaf man, watching the parade from an overpass under which the motorcade had just shot, saw a man in the parking lot throw a rifle to another man, who dismantled it before putting it into a car. When he tried to tell the police, his account was rebuffed.

Many of the crowd now ran up the mound, having heard loud bangs and seen and smelt gun smoke drifting out from under the trees in front of the fence behind them. As they did so, the umbrella man casually joined a Cuban-looking fellow and sat down nonchalantly on the kerb beside him.

Other witnesses said they had heard shots coming from a building behind the president, the Texas School Book Depository, and had seen at least two men at an open sixth-floor window, one holding a long gun. Police entered the building, where they found a discarded high-powered but crappy rifle with a defective sight and an arrangement of boxes beside the window in question.

Kennedy had now arrived at Parkland Hospital, where nurse Audrey Parker was on duty. She carefully described the throat wound: 'It looked small and round like an entry wound, instead of larger like an exit wound could often look.' But more gruesome than this, a great lump of JFK's head on the back right had been blown out behind him. Beyond help, President John Fitzgerald Kennedy was pronounced dead at exactly 1 p.m. Dallas time. Vice President Lyndon Johnson was quickly sworn in as the new president, in the cramped cabin of the presidential plane. As he took the oath his friend and fellow politician Ralph Thomas was photographed winking at him.

A young man was soon arrested on suspicion of the assassination. He was named as Lee Harvey Oswald, who was said to be a Marxist troublemaker and ex-defector, who worked at the Texas School Book Depository building. He maintained throughout his questioning that he had shot nobody.

While he was still safely in police custody at Dallas Police Headquarters Oswald was shot and killed by a local man named Jack Ruby, who had been let into the building. Lee Harvey Oswald could not now be tried for the president's murder, and the idea was quickly established that there was nobody else firing guns in Dealey Plaza that day. He was the 'lone-nut gunman'. All the same, as he was never found guilty, or even tried in court, we ought to presume his innocence.

In the days to come, many odd things continued to happen. On the orders of LBJ, Kennedy's limousine was dismantled, refurbished and thoroughly cleaned. Its windscreen, which contained a bullet hole, was removed and destroyed. An expert in bullet holes in glass, who had examined it before its destruction, explained that the bullet had come in from the front. The vehicle was now of little use as evidence. Bloodstained clothes were likewise laundered, with similar effect. In due course President Kennedy's brain disappeared.

In fact, it wasn't long before a stream of evidence sprang up pointing to something very fishy having gone on, and doubts began to emerge about the official story. For example, Jack Ruby, a dingy-nightclub owner with strong links to the Mob, knew Oswald well and the pair had repeatedly been seen together in Ruby's place, though the press forgot to mention this.

Oswald couldn't have been more different from Ruby, being a slim, well-spoken former Marine who had worked at the CIA's U-2 spy-plane base in Japan and been trained in Russian – probably at the US Defense

Language Institute in Monterey, California. When he suddenly defected to the Soviet Union in 1959, Russians were struck by his fluency.

After a couple of years living the high life in Minsk, the traitor decided to return to the States. He was not arrested, or questioned about his defection, but warmly greeted on arrival by a rabidly anti-communist gentleman with intelligence connections. He was waved through immigration with his new Russian wife, and given a loan by the American government.

Oswald now moved to Fort Worth, Texas, where he landed a job at a company that handled secret maps for the Army, with no worries about his 'defection'. He began hanging around not with fellow Marxists but with members of the well-heeled anti-Soviet Russian *émigré* community in Dallas, including a rich anti-communist Russian CIA asset with strong ties to Dallas oil millionaires, who had become the Marxist's best friend, though he was some three decades his senior.

Whatever he actually was, Oswald seems to have been thoroughly manipulated for some time before the assassination. Indeed, there is every sign that his various minders and 'friends' had been keeping tabs on him as he was nudged into the position of 'patsy', which is exactly what he told the press he was. Whether he shot anyone that day in Dallas is doubtful.

In the end the people who pulled the triggers and waved the umbrellas are small fry. According to testimony by Madeleine Duncan Brown, the long-time mistress of Lyndon Johnson, the night before the assassination there had been a significant meeting during a party at the Dallas home of oil millionaire Clint Murchison Sr. This consisted of what Brown referred to as 'a close-knitted group' of influential men, including H. L. Hunt (multi-millionaire oil magnate), Lyndon Johnson (vice president), J. Edgar Hoover (neighbour and dinner guest of LBJ, and head of the FBI), Richard Nixon (sometime vice president and future president), Charles P. Cabell, fired by Kennedy as deputy director of the CIA after the failed Cuba invasion), John McCloy (lawyer, banker, intelligence man and so-called 'Chairman of the American Establishment'), Jack Ruby and George Brown (of Brown and Root, the defence contractor that did so well out of the Vietnam War and later became part of Halliburton, which did so well out of the Iraq War). Brown was a great chum and sometime roommate of Ralph Thomas, the man who would be photographed winking at LBJ at his swearing-in. He was also a pal of Oswald's Russian *émigré* friend. Coming out of this meeting, Johnson, who loathed both JFK and his brother, Attorney General Bobby Kennedy, told Madeleine Duncan Brown: 'After tomorrow, those goddamn Kennedys will never embarrass me again. That's no threat, that's a promise.' She added that, three months later, LBJ confirmed to her in a hotel that the conspiracy to kill Kennedy had been the responsibility of 'Texas oilmen' and what he called 'renegade intelligence bastards in Washington'. He forgot to mention his own loathing of Kennedy, and his burning desire to be president.

From the outset, Kennedy had upset many influential people by being a smooth, educated northerner, and had alarmed others by deciding on 2 October 1963 to withdraw US forces from Vietnam, threatening to 'splinter the CIA into a thousand pieces and scatter it into the wind', softening the aggressive stance towards Castro's Cuba and the USSR, and vowing to crack down on organised crime, fire J. Edgar Hoover and greatly increase oil industry taxes. It is also worth noting that JFK's secretary, Evelyn Lincoln, reported a 'persistent rumour' going around in the autumn of 1963 that Kennedy was planning to drop Lyndon Johnson from the ticket in 1964.

The members of this cabal of oil millionaires, intelligence and Mob types, politicians, publishers, military contractors and money men had strong political, and sometimes personal, motives for wanting Kennedy out and Johnson in. They all knew each other, and had a great deal of money, as well as numerous political, criminal, military, media, CIA, FBI and police connections. The setting was perfect, for the South was also home to the Kennedy-hating, anti-Castro Cubans: just the place for the conspiracy to be planned and executed.

A well-oiled assassination conspiracy of this magnitude needs only a very few people at its heart. But they must be powerful: they must control the story, organise the cover-up, pay for but not dirty their hands with the nitty-gritty of the actual killing, arrange for the sacrifice of a distracting fall guy or 'patsy', get the police and media on board, destroy incriminating evidence, ignore witnesses telling the wrong story and shut down any proper press inquiry. And they must prevail. This is not hard if you are motivated, powerful, very well connected and extremely rich.

Most of the American public distrust the official explanation of what happened in Dallas that day in 1963, and fewer than a third think Oswald was the 'lone gunman', firing a defective rifle with world-class accuracy from a privately owned building behind the president. Since the day of Oswald's murder, the mantra of the mass media has always been that we will probably never know what happened, that the truth about events of this significance is beyond our feeble ability to understand. From the mainstream media there has been, save for a few brave exceptions, hardly a flicker of inquiry into the gross suspiciousness of these events. Instead, a dedicated community of assassination researchers has spent decades digging up endless evidence of official deception at the highest levels. One of these persistent enquirers explained his motivation for the years of toil: 'I just never could understand how you could be shot in the front from the back.'

Some of these researchers are obsessive, some are mediocre, but a good many are very bright and extremely good at what they do. Together they have uncovered a deeply troubling picture, and posed some big questions that have yet to be answered by those who know. For all of them the official media reserves that single, very effective dismissal phrase: 'conspiracy nut'.

In 1976, after years of resistance, the US government did reluctantly order an inquiry into the assassination, finally concluding that *more than one person probably was involved* in the killing of President Kennedy. Thus, representatives of the US government finally declared themselves the most official conspiracy nuts ever.

II

IS ANYBODY OUT THERE?

UFO and Alien Conspiracy Theories

We are never deceived;
we deceive ourselves.

—GOETHE

The Roswell Incident

On Tuesday, 8 July 1947, an officer of Roswell Army Air Field (RAAF), New Mexico, issued a press release announcing that the 509th Operations Group had recovered a 'flying disc' that had crashed near the town. The next morning, the *Roswell Daily Record* splashed a brash headline across its front page: RAAF CAPTURES FLYING SAUCER ON RANCH IN ROSWELL REGION. The story explained how, about three weeks previously, on 14 June, foreman William Brazel and his eight-year-old son had noticed strange pieces of debris scattered around the ranch he ran, some thirty miles north of Roswell. The paper said that Brazel had seen a 'large area of bright wreckage made up of rubber strips, tinfoil, a rather tough paper and sticks', and had gathered up the remains with his family on 4 July. In all, he reckoned the material probably weighed about 5 lb (2 kg).

On 24 June, just ten days after Brazel's discovery, and a mere fortnight before the *Daily Record*'s splash, amateur pilot Kenneth Arnold told a reporter about strange lights he had seen scooting across the sky. They moved, he said, 'like a saucer if you skip it across the water'. The reporter, being a reporter, decided this meant they were saucer-shaped, and before you could say 'slow news day', headline writers were referring to these objects as 'flying saucers'. This was the first use of the term.

Brazel thought this might be what he had discovered, and on 6 or 7 July – Roswell dates have been vague from the start – he whispered his suspicion 'kinda confidential like' to a local sheriff, who contacted RAAF major Jesse Marcel. Marcel visited the ranch and tracked down a few more 'patches of tinfoil and rubber'.

Then, on Thursday, 10 July, the *Record* gave further details: no metal or propellers had been found, although a paper fin was discovered glued to the foil. The paper had eyelets in it, suggesting some sort of attachment, and, most intriguingly, there were letters on some of the fragments, though no complete words. There was also evidence of Scotch tape and 'some tape with flowers printed upon it'. If this was a flying saucer, it was engineered from rather chintzy materials.

The bits and pieces of the unidentified object were flown to Fort Worth Army Air Field, where they were again identified as just a 'weather balloon' along with its 'kite', a kind of radar reflector.

The boring 'truth' having been revealed, the 'flying saucer' story fizzled out and people got on with their lives. But, unknown to the public, the facts were quite different.

It was another three decades before a 'UFO researcher' gave the story the kiss of life, prompting a series of elaborate conspiracy theories featuring extraterrestrial corpses, secret military operations, a sinister disinformation programme and alien autopsies of the third kind. UFO researchers had uncovered a multitude of witnesses with interesting stories to tell, and people were waking up to what was to become the most famous UFO sighting of all time.

Reports were now coming out that at least one alien spaceship had crashed at the Roswell ranch and that extraterrestrial pilots, as well as alien corpses, had been captured by the military. Apparently, the ET craft had been observing US nuclear-weapons testing but had crashed after a lightning strike that killed all on board. A government cover-up, it was said, naturally followed.

Major Jesse Marcel, the intelligence officer who had first recovered debris from the site, was now describing the remains as 'nothing made on this earth', backed up by a neighbour and William Brazel's own son. The conclusion was that newspaper photographs of the time, showing Marcel posing with innocuous bits and pieces from a weather balloon, had been substituted for pictures showing the actual debris. This looked like an official cover-up to discredit the growing public curiosity about flying saucers, which, if it really was a cover-up, would continue to work for thirty years.

It was in 1989 that the first reports of Roswell alien autopsies emerged. These bodies, it was claimed, had even been seen by President Eisenhower. But there were doubts. There always are doubts. It was said that in the three or four decades since the event, many memories had become hazy or muddled. Major Marcel, for instance, turned out to have incorrectly remembered being decorated for shooting down enemy planes. But we all make mistakes like this, *don't we*? All the same, the confusing array of contradictory stories was causing even UFO researchers to become irritated with each other. It was a classic case of quantity over quality.

In fact, the differing UFO conspiracy theories masked something much more interesting, rich and strange. It has now been admitted that there was indeed a government conspiracy going on, one designed to hide exactly what had really happened at Roswell on that fateful day.

Between 1947 and 1949 the US Army Air Forces had been running a top-secret programme called Project Mogul. This was a secret part of an unclassified New York University research project being carried out by atmosphere scientists, in which microphones were flown on high-altitude balloons so as to pick up sound waves from Soviet atomic bomb tests. The debris discovered by William Brazel at Roswell was most likely from Project Mogul balloon NYU Flight 4, launched on 4 June 1947, ten days before Brazel's discovery of the wreckage.

The military had decided to switch off public interest in the apparatus by concealing the true nature of the Roswell incident, blandly remarking that the bits and pieces from the crashed object, seen at their press conference, were the remnants of a boring weather balloon. This strategy was highly successful and all interest in the story withered away for three decades.

Naturally enough, however, UFO researchers dismissed the Project Mogul explanation as implausible Air Force disinformation.

Men in Black

On 21 June 1947, at the height of the American post-war UFO scare, Fred Crisman and Harold Dahl – who said they were harbour patrolmen working near Maury Island, an islet in Puget Sound, on the West Coast of the USA – told how they were operating their boat when they spotted something strange in the sky above them. They described six ring-doughnut-shaped objects, one of which dropped something resembling white metal or lava onto the boat, breaking the arm of a colleague and killing a dog.

Crisman and Dahl explained their experience to an amateur pilot named Kenneth Arnold, who, just three days later, curiously enough, had his own flying-saucer encounter at nearby Mount Rainier. Arnold arranged for two Air Force intelligence officers to fly in to investigate the Maury Island incident. They quickly identified the substance said to have been dropped by the UFOs. It was, they said, earthly aluminium, which they described, rather coolly, as being of no interest. But on their return flight from this less-than-dazzling trip their B-25 caught fire and crashed, killing both men. The coincidence seemed too convenient and some suggested they had perished because they 'knew too much'. But if this was so, who had done them in?

Dahl told how, following these events, he had been approached by a man in a dark suit, who forbade him to discuss the strange occurrences. 'I know a great deal more about this experience of yours than you will want to believe,' said the stranger.

The forbidding appearance of this darkly dressed man was not, however, a unique affair. A few short years later a prominent UFO researcher named Albert K. Bender outlined the way he too had been visited at home by three men in dark suits. They flashed credentials before telling him 'sternly and emphatically' to shut down his investigations into flying saucers. Bender explained that these Men in Black were secret government agents whose job it was to muzzle all talk of UFOs.

Soon the presence of MIB, as they came to be known, was being reported everywhere, though cameras failed to capture them. Witnesses described them as always wearing black suits, and said they would typically warn or harass their subjects, rather like a social worker. Sometimes, it was claimed, they would even kill them. It was said they worked for secretive unknown organisations or for various branches of government, usually the CIA or FBI, and almost never the Department of Agriculture, or the bit that keeps the libraries going.

Was it true that the government was spying on its citizens? An analysis of Project Blue Book, a study of unidentified flying objects carried out by the US Air Force in the fifties and sixties, noted darkly that UFO organisations 'should be watched because of their potentially great influence on mass thinking if widespread sightings should occur'. It murmured suspiciously about 'subversive purposes'.

UFO spotters were well aware that Air Force personnel were being sent out to interview them officially, so it is hardly surprising that Men in Black surfaced as such a compelling conspiracy theory. Could the interviewers be the good cops and the Men in Black the bad cops?

These men were frequently described as large, tall or dominating, and they often appeared to have unusual faces. Their eyes were apt to be concealed behind dark glasses and they would sometimes lack eyebrows or fingernails, or have weirdly plastic-looking skin. This led to another theory: might they themselves be aliens? It would all fit. Noted ufologist John Keel, who helped to popularise the term 'Men in Black', said he had been approached by such swarthy 'demonic supernaturals', who had dark skin and 'exotic' facial features. The similarity of this description to trite racial slurs did not go unremarked.

It is interesting to note that in Western cultures black – a light-absorbing hue – confers great authority on its wearers, not to say an element of dread. Priestly vestments, vampires' cloaks, official cars, academic gowns, barristers' and undertakers' outfits and the suits of presidential bodyguards are predominantly black. Witches too use the colour to their advantage. It is no surprise, then, to learn of the alarm provoked by the sudden appearance of a stern, expressionless figure in black togs, warning you to obey his sinister instructions. Imagine the same fellow kitted out in pink, with a cashmere shawl around his shoulders. Not the same thing at all.

But what of Fred 'flying doughnuts' Crisman? In an extraordinary parallel to his UFO reports, Fred's name popped up again in December 1968, when he was identified – incorrectly as it turned out – as one of three mysterious 'hoboes' arrested and photographed in Dallas, soon after the shooting of President John F. Kennedy.

But this misapprehension was not the only one surrounding Crisman. One day, he and Dahl – who had received the creepy Man-in-Black visit – blandly announced that they had simply made up the whole Maury Island story. This came as a shock to investigators. How is anyone to know what to believe if people just start inventing things? Being naturally sceptical, ufologists didn't accept Dahl and Crisman's about-turn. Was it not more likely that pressure from the Men in Black had had its intended effect, and shut down the truth?

Actually, the truth was even stranger, because Albert Bender now remarked that he too had had other ideas. The visit to his home by the three Men in Black, he said, had been a mental rather than physical visit. He explained that he had made an astral projection to their secret headquarters in Antarctica, adding for fullness of disclosure that the Men in Black came in three genders, rather like German nouns. You might have thought that, to everyone but the most zealous proponent, all this wavering would have put the kibosh on the Men-in-Black conspiracy theory. But no, it still has its firm believers. And who can say they are wrong?

Area 51

Hidden away in a parched corner of the roasting Nevada desert, inhospitable to everything but the giant hairy scorpion, deadly diamondbacks and the occasional thirsty Gila monster, lies the vast, crinkled disc of Groom Lake. Ringed by a mountainous wilderness, this great dry salt flat is surrounded on every side by the sprawling expanse of the Nellis Air Force Base 'bombing and gunnery range'. Its formidable perimeter is dotted with seismic motion detectors and cocksure security cameras that record any unwelcome approach by curiosity seekers. Shouty NO TRESPASSING signs in red capitals caution the nosey that this is a RESTRICTED AREA and that photography is prohibited. In smaller print towards the foot of the signs is the mild warning: 'Use of deadly force authorized'. Any rubberneckers who wander too close up the dirt roads that approach the range are apt to be surprised by the sudden appearance of white vans containing chunky gentlemen in camouflage gear and aggressive sunglasses, who will politely appeal to un-invited guests to 'Get the fuck outta here!' while encouragingly waving around king-size black guns. Though the airspace above the range is restricted for miles around, and high into the atmosphere, a few satellite photographs do exist, including some taken by the Russians, along with some snaps from the edge of the no-fly zone. These show the hard, white surface of Groom Lake, like a huge potato crisp crisscrossed by monster runways, flanked by sinister grey-white hangars and military-style service buildings. Everything here is BIG.

The US government claims that 'Area 51' is a name that has never been officially used, though it appears – surprise, surprise – in a CIA document from Cold War days. The area is also known as The Site, The Box, Dreamland, Watertown, Paradise Ranch and, most boringly, Homey Airport.

The extreme secrecy and government touchiness that surround this area have led to an explosion of conspiracy theories about what exactly goes on there. Activities are said to include the development of laser, microwave and particle-beam weaponry, weather-control experiments (*see page 93*), the secret development of captured Nazi weapons, time travel and teleportation R&D, and projects related to 'Majestic 12' (MJ-12), the codename of a secret committee of scientists, military men and government officials apparently formed in 1947 by President Truman for the investigation and recovery of alien spaceships. It is also said that some people who have got too close to Area 51 have been seized, never to be heard of again. It goes without saying that Area 51 is also claimed to be home to secret one-world-government enterprises.

Most notoriously, a link between Area 51 and myster-ies around the 1947 crash of an unidentified flying object in Roswell, New Mexico (*see page 29*), led theorists to conclude that the bodies of dead aliens had been taken to Area 51, where they were studied and dissected. There was also talk of secret joint enterprises with living extraterrestrials.

These conspiracy theories were given a huge boost in 1995 when some creepy handheld black-and-white film, said to have been recorded at the time of the Roswell incident, appeared on television. This spine-tingling footage, though fuzzy, showed what appeared to be government agents conducting a grisly post-mortem on the lifeless body of one of the alien beings. The subsequent announcement by a man claiming to be the film's producer that it was not original film but mostly a reconstruction did not convince everyone. Indeed, there are people who still maintain that living extraterrestrials are kept in Area-51, including a few who are held hostage.

So pervasive is the multitude of flying-saucer stories that state officials have chosen to dub the nearby Route 375 the 'Extraterrestrial Highway', causing absolutely no harm to local tourism. The surrounding territory is now a popular destination for ufologists, where observers have long reported sighting unidentified flying objects and other alien shenanigans.

It was only in 1989 that the full range of Area 51's true goings-on actually came out. An interesting fellow called Bob Lazar, with degrees, apparently, from the California Institute of Technology (Caltech) and the Massachusetts Institute of Technology (MIT), emerged from the shadows to explain that, at the height of these strange and secret activities, he had been hired as a civilian engineer to work at a clandestine underground site named 'S-4', some miles south of Area 51.

Despite the obsessive government secrecy, Lazar spoke forthrightly, in numerous television interviews, about all he had been doing. He said he had seen government documents describing alien visits to Earth going back ten thousand years, and had been instructed to examine a captured flying saucer so as to reverse-engineer the alien spacecraft's gravitational propulsion system.

Bob Lazar's breathtaking revelations, alongside the weirdness of the Area 51 site and bucketloads of government secrecy, have naturally made it the pole star of a whole variety of UFO and other conspiracy theories. There is said to be a transcontinental underground railway beneath the desert sand, and a vanishing runway known as 'Cheshire Airstrip', which becomes visible only when water is sprayed onto its cleverly cloaked surface, appearing and disappearing like Lewis Carroll's Cheshire cat.

But though Bob Lazar's technical descriptions sounded highly plausible, physicists and engineers who heard him were puzzled. Bob seemed to have confused gravity with particles, and had also got in a bit of a muddle with anti-matter – which anyone might do, I suppose. Ufologists themselves became uneasy, however, when it was revealed that neither Caltech nor MIT could find any record of Lazar on their books. It was only a few months later that the wheels finally came off, when Lazar was convicted of involvement in a prostitution caper, thus setting back Area-51 research by decades.

Bob Lazar faded to black as a reliable spokesman, but you can't keep a good man down, and just as his curious goings-on with ladies of the night were vanishing from memory he bobbed up again. In a 2018 film he reminisced about walking down a hallway in the old days back at 'S-4'. He recalled looking through a small window and getting a flash of two lab-coated gentlemen together with a small, grey alien creature. Lazar said he was told by a guard to pay no attention and to move along. The jury is still out on this one.

It's so difficult to get to the bottom of even the simplest Area-51 puzzle but I decided to have a go. I thought I would start with the basics and calculate the distance from Roswell, New Mexico – site of the mysterious 1947 discovery of crashed UFO debris – to Groom Lake. One source gave me a distance of 893 miles between the two, which looks about right from the map, but who knows? Girding my loins, I put the details into my favourite online map app and … nothing happened. Well, that's not quite true: *something* happened, and it was very strange. Though no distance results were served up, I got this enigmatic message: 'Sorry, we could not calculate driving directions from "Roswell, New Mexico, USA" to "Groom Lake, Nevada, USA". Now get lost!' OK, it didn't actually say, 'Now get lost!' but it might just as well have done.

To find out whether it was a mapping error, I tried the distance to Roswell from a totally innocuous town in a totally innocuous state – Bismarck, North Dakota – with this result: 'DELAYS: Moderate traffic in this area.'

So no worries about Bismarck, ND, then, or Roswell, NM. Now it was time for my master plan: to try to get the distance from harmless Bismarck to mysterious Groom Lake (Area 51), and guess what? – I got this: 'Sorry, we could not calculate driving directions from "Bismarck, North Dakota, USA" to "Groom Lake, Nevada, USA".' So, it *was* Area 51 that was the trouble. Why the secrecy?

Well, together with the alien-spacecraft business, there is a claim among some conspiracy-theory supporters that Area 51 is really home to the government's so-called 'black helicopter' programme (*see page 169*), and also that they have conducted tests into secret aircraft, including the Lockheed SR-71 *Blackbird*, a scary-looking high-altitude supersonic spy plane developed as a black project during the Cold War, by Lockheed's so-called 'Skunk Works', an official nickname for their more blandly titled 'Advanced Development Programs'.

These claims of secret aircraft tests do not convince hardened flying-saucer conspiracy supporters but they are getting extremely warm.

In the mid-1950s, a number of reports began coming in to the government from commercial airline captains who were noticing the increasingly common presence of unidentified flying objects in the skies above them. Unknown to these pilots, the Lockheed U-2 spy plane, nicknamed *Dragon Lady*, had recently begun secret test flights at more than 60,000 feet, roughly twice the flying height of commercial planes. Going west during the early evening, these pilots might see the setting sun bouncing off the body of the U-2, creating what some said was a 'fiery' look.

A later spy plane, the Lockheed A-12 *Oxcart*, had a weird fuselage, designed to carry enormous amounts of fuel. Its highly unusual and militarily distinctive anatomy made it unforgettable. Airline pilots looking up from their cardboard coffee and reheated Chicken Surprise would see high above them the sparkling metallic underside of *Oxcart* as it shot overhead like a bullet, at 2,000 mph, its titanium body reflecting the sun, convincing them that aliens were on the warpath.

Many of these reports were checked by the Air Force's Project Blue Book, one of a series of investigations that lasted from 1952 until 1970. After exhaustive searches they decided there was 'no evidence indicating that sightings categorized as "unidentified" were extraterrestrial vehicles'. It was the U-2 that accounted for most of the reports, though the Air Force could not reveal the truth. In fact, they concluded that the rumours might help keep Area 51's true operations a secret.

Top-secret 'black-program' testing of new aircraft continued at Area 51 until 1981, the most secret planes being moved in and out at night, and in bits, in huge military transport aircraft. In 1967 a Soviet MiG-21 was delivered into US hands by a defector and was taken in great secrecy to Groom Lake where, in the amusingly codenamed 'Have Doughnut' project, it was flown in simulated combat. To prevent sightings, the zone above the range was closed, being marked on maps in red ink, thus leading to another Area 51 nickname: 'Red Square'.

Still, despite all the signs with the base's name on them, and the friendly tour guides in the white vans, it was not until 2013, in grudging response to a freedom of information request put in eight years earlier, that the CIA finally agreed that the site was actually a thing. Russia may already have known all this but you don't want to rush into these things with your own people. The government now admits that Area 51 is actually the Nevada Test and Training Range, designated 'Area 51' on a map when they acquired it. First used during the Second World War as a gunnery range for army pilots, the area was developed in extreme secrecy in 1955 by Lockheed design boss Kelly Johnson for the testing of his U-2. In fact, Johnson described the dry lakebed of Groom Lake as 'a perfect natural landing field ... as smooth as a billiard table without anything being done to it', the mountains providing a handy natural barrier to unwelcome visitors. The area has since been used for bombing practice, wargame exercises and nuclear tests.

On 20 September 2019, a Facebook event took place which aimed to find alien life by storming Area 51. Imaginatively named 'Storm Area 51, They Can't Stop All of Us', it caused more than two million people to click the Facebook 'Going' button, and another million and a half to click 'Interested'. On the day, however, only about 150 people showed up, and, not surprisingly, none got in. That means that some 1,999,850 people who said they were coming to the do didn't bother, which is a dropout rate worth remembering next time you have invited your Facebook friends to a party and are trying to calculate how many sausages you will need.

As so often happens with these things, the creator, Matty Roberts, was taken aback by the response, having invented the idea as a joke. He said that at first he received a measly forty replies, but to his surprise the event suddenly went viral, becoming an internet meme that spread to other social media. Roberts explained that he was so stupefied by all this that he expected a visit from the FBI to find out what he was up to.

Having been tipped off to the meme, the authorities issued a veiled warning, in an attempt to discourage visitors. A government spokeswoman described Area 51 as: 'an open training range ... where we train American armed forces. The US Air Force always stands ready to protect America and its assets.'

At least, that is the way they would like to explain it ...

III

DEAD MEN WALKING

Dubious Deaths and Dodgy Doppelgangers

There are two ways to be fooled. One is to believe what isn't true; the other is to refuse to believe what is true.

—SØREN KIERKEGAARD

Conspiracy Theorist Alex Jones Is Actually Bill Hicks

Born in 1974, Alex Jones is a self-styled libertarian conservative, a so-called 'gun nut' and America's leading conspiracy theorist. He has his own conspiracy theory website – InfoWars – and hosts the syndicated *Alex Jones Show* on US radio. Jones, who says he is 'proud to be listed as a thought criminal against Big Brother', thinks the US government plans to turn people homosexual with chemicals, and backs the idea that it was behind the Oklahoma City bombing and was also mixed up in the 1969 'fake' Moon landings (*see page 116*).

Alex Jones has covered all the favourite American conspiracy theories, but there is one he is not so keen on, but which he can neither defend nor attack without reinforcing it. This theory says that Alex Jones is not Alex Jones but is actually the cult Texas comedian Bill Hicks, who died – *or is said to have done* – in 1994 at the age of just thirty-two, though, interestingly, he had no public funeral. It is alleged in a YouTube video that looks into this subject that Hicks was recruited by the CIA to 'become the controlled opposition by the mainstream media', and was 'continuously fed approved intelligence by his CIA handlers'. This might be true, except that I have no idea what it means.

Bill Hicks was not a Texas native but moved there as a young man, attending Stratford High School. Alex Jones claims he attended a different school, Anderson High, though it is said he actually has no verifiable history before 1994. *Interesting.* It is claimed that when people ring to check, Anderson High School denies having any record of him. I have to confess I decided not to look deeply into this assertion because I thought the head teacher was probably sick to death of being phoned up at all hours with demands for him or her to confirm or deny that Alexander Emerick (or Emric) Jones once picked his nose at the back of some teacher's class there.

After school, Bill Hicks became a spiky stand-up comedian. He was a particular critic of US wars, religion and the Republican Party, and made frequent satirical or jocular remarks about drug taking, social conformity and autofellatio. Hicks also told jokes about conspiracy theories, including the one concerning the Kennedy assassination (*see page 18*), which he was convinced was true. He even faked his own murder on stage, to show the insidious purpose of governments who assassinate those who threaten their interests.

Hicks was especially popular in the UK in the early nineties, but died – it is claimed – in 1994 from pancreatic cancer that had spread to his liver. In the years after his death his albums developed a cult following and he even made it to No. 4 on Channel 4's '100 Greatest Stand-up Comics' list.

But did he really die?

I have read that the so-called 'powers that be' might have got to Bill and somehow forced him to work for them by, say, offering to cure his cancer if he agreed to 'die' and be reborn as Alex. This sounds an interesting idea, but what might their motive have been? And if they have found a cure for pancreatic cancer, why aren't they out there making a fortune from it instead of keeping it under their hats?

The trouble is that the theory that Alex Jones is not Alex Jones but actually Bill Hicks is a hard one for Jones either to confirm or deny. If he rubbishes the theory people will say he is naturally denying it because it is true, and who would know the truth about the fake Alex Jones better than the real Bill Hicks? If he promotes it, his reputation for backing unsubstantiated theories will be held against him. He has, for example, had to repudiate, and apologise for supporting, 'Pizzagate', a 2016 conspiracy theory that wrongly linked the Clinton Foundation, human trafficking and a pizza restaurant (*see page 210*).

There is no doubt that at the time Bill 'died', which was before Alex got more rotund and elderly looking, they did indeed resemble each other. Even at that young age, both were already rather paunchy white gentlemen with chubby cheeks, small chins and pronounced nasolabial folds – the creases that run from your nose to the corners of your mouth. They also had similar-looking eyes, eyebrows and teeth, or possibly *tooth caps*. These days Jones no longer has much hair, which I think makes him look a lot older than he is, as well he might if he is really Bill Hicks. He claims to have been born in 1974, while Bill Hicks was born in 1961 – thirteen years earlier.

The strange thing is, though, that if Alex Jones really is Bill Hicks, he has changed his political viewpoint dramatically, though he has retained the distinctive ranty style that he shared with Hicks, or, perhaps, that he shared with himself. All the same, back when Hicks was at his height, he and Jones were shouting from opposite sides of the political canyon. It's true that many left-wing politicians end up wearing cardigans and sucking Werther's Originals, snoozing away their pensions in the House of Lords, as Lord Rednose or Lady Gyntime. It's conceivable that Hicks's firebrand politics turned around with time, so that instead of ranting about war he is now a gun freak. Though the two men appear politically different, there is a sameness in their anti-establishment cores. They both back/backed the central idea, for example, that the government is there to make you unthinkingly accept all the garbage it pumps out to benefit nobody but itself.

To see whether you can tell the two men apart, try and spot which of these quotes is by left-wing flag-waver 'Bill Hicks' and which by right-wing tub-thumper 'Alex Jones':

'Madison Avenue makes us addicts of consumerism.'

'I have the government documents where they said they're going to encourage homosexuality with chemicals so that people don't have children.'

ALEX JONES IS ACTUALLY BILL HICKS

'Mainstream media is the enemy.'
'The majority of frogs in most areas of the United
    States are now gay.'

Guess what? – they are all Jones.

The Cloning of Avril Lavigne

In 1998, a fourteen-year-old French-Canadian girl named Avril Lavigne won a singing contest that started her on a journey towards musical stardom.

Fourteen years later, in 2012, a curious report began circulating about this world-shakingly successful blonde singer-songwriter. The story had begun on a Brazilian Portuguese-language blog, '*Avril Esta Morta*' ('Avril Is Dead'), which reported that the singer with the big blue eyes and good bone structure had supposedly died and been reincarnated as a clone.

The claim went this way: at the start of her career Avril had struggled to come to terms with sudden fame and had hired a young woman named Melissa Vandella as a lookalike paparazzi-distracter. Then, in 2003, aged just eighteen, the tattooed 'Sk8er Boi' artiste had suffered a bout of depression, shortly after the death of her much-loved grandfather and the blockbuster success of her seminal debut album, the ominously titled *Let Go*. The new superstar had then been found dead at her home, having hanged herself. This was a massive blow for her label, so, in an old-fashioned industry conspiracy, the record company and others simply decided to replace her.

Lookalike Melissa was ideal for the job: she had spent so much time observing and absorbing Avril's mannerisms that she was already a clone of the real thing. Melissa agreed to go along with the ruse and Avril's family hushed it up.

Evidence for the switcheroo, it is said, included the artist's stylish red-carpet photographs, in which the differences between Avril and Melissa couldn't be clearer. The real Avril prefers trousers, while Melissa generally goes for skirts and dresses. There is even one photograph in which the daring doppelganger has 'MELISSA' boldly written on her hand.

Visible differences in close-ups of her face between 2003 and today are another apparent giveaway. Since the switch, subtle and not-so-subtle changes have become noticeable. What else could possibly explain these alterations other than reincarnation as a clone? Sceptics point out that the singer is now twice the age she was when she was first photographed and her face has naturally changed as she has developed. But conspiracy theorists are unpersuaded by such obvious excuses. What's more, pictures showing the freckles on Lavigne's bare arms indicate that the singer has fewer of them now than she did before 2003, when her double took over. *Amazing*.

As well as Lavigne's physical appearance, there have been claims that her musical style has changed since her clone began depping her gigs. This is a tricky one. If you compare the Beatles' first hit, 'Love Me Do' (1962), with 'Let It Be' (1970), just eight years later, you'll clearly hear the difference in musical style. So, whether any change in Avril's groove is down to artistic progression or her now being a completely different person is impossible to say for sure.

But there are clues too in her songs' lyrics, which seem to refer to the death of the real Avril Lavigne. Such phrases as: 'The day you slipped away', 'I can't bring you back', 'You are gone' and 'It won't be the same' couldn't be plainer in their real meaning. Someone was clearly trying to send a message …

In 2018, replying to a journalist's question about what it was like to be a clone, Avril said, 'Yeah, some people think that I'm not the real me, *which is so weird*. Like, why would they even think that?' But this is *exactly* what a clone would say, isn't it!

The Avril Lavigne conspiracy theory is still popular on social media and in pub quizzes, and rumours have continued to buzz, even after an astonishing announcement, three years after his original posting, by the author of the original 2015 '*Avril Esta Morta*'. In this message he said he had fabricated the whole thing, and claimed to have put up the blog as an experiment into the way conspiracy theories take off on the internet, with some people believing everything they read or hear. 'I created this theory to see if people would believe it,' said the jolly japer, 'and thousands of people believed it was a fact.' But Avril Lavigne had not died, he said, and was never replaced by a lookalike. 'I apologise to people who believed that she was dead … it was all just a theory created by me.'

But where is the evidence that this itself is not a fabrication? Maybe the blog's author is himself a clone. Just think: it could go on for ever.

The Return of the King

Elvis Presley, the sleek and handsome twentieth-century music phenomenon, was known as the 'King of Rock and Roll' as much for his sexually provocative performances as for his singing. One showbiz colleague, struck by the thrusting pelvis, said he 'perceived a soda bottle in Presley's trousers'.

But Elvis the Pelvis wasn't looking after himself properly and by the age of thirty-eight his health was seriously ropey. His diet was a monotonous stream of foot-long bacon, peanut butter and jam rolls supplemented by hamburgers and fried bread. He was badly overweight and suffering from diabetes, high blood pressure, glaucoma, liver damage, an enlarged colon and chronic constipation. Many of these complaints were exacerbated by sustained drug abuse. In 1973, he was taken to hospital semi-comatose, having twice overdosed on barbiturates, and one year he was prescribed 10,000 doses of pick-me-ups and put-me-to-sleeps before the first leaf had fallen from the southern tulip tree.

Despite his failing health, Elvis was a hard worker: there were 168 concerts in his 1974 tour. But these were strange dos, attended largely by middle-aged ladies with blue hair. A musician who worked on these shows described Elvis as 'all gut', his voice so slurred that the songs were barely intelligible. During introductions he clung to the microphone stand, a bleary, sequinned cartoon of his previous sexy self.

When not touring, Presley spent his days in his Memphis mansion, a sort of French farmhouse affair with a gigantic neoclassical pediment and columns nailed on the front. Here, between cholesterol-rich sandwiches, he read books on spiritualism or recited *Monty Python* sketches to visitors.

Then, on 16 August 1977, the eve of his latest tour, Elvis's girlfriend, Ginger Alden, found him unresponsive on the bathroom floor. He had been sitting on the toilet and had fallen forward directly in front of it, she said, 'completely frozen' in a seated position. He never regained consciousness and was pronounced dead on the steps of the Baptist Hospital, Memphis, aged just forty-two. A post-mortem revealed traces of fourteen drugs in his system.

One result of Presley's unstinting opioid abuse and a diet rich in rubbish was his chronic constipation. This, it was proposed, might have led to a recognised effect: the so-called 'Valsalva manoeuvre', in which, while 'straining at stool', the abdominal aorta is so compressed that it causes the heart to stop.

Elvis was buried at Graceland, beside his mother. Yet even as the tears were drying on the pillows of his millions of fans, the idea began circulating that the King was not really dead. Conspiracists said that, having wearied of the spotlight and desperately wanting to escape it, he had decided not to retire but to fake his own death. What he settled on, it seemed, was getting a helicopter to land on the Graceland lawn, where he hopped aboard to be flown to Bermuda. There he blended at once into the background, totally unrecognised. This theory did not say who the toilet-side crouching corpse was, or who they had buried in Graceland's back yard, or why his girlfriend had gone along with the scheme. These were mere details.

The key lay perhaps in a mysterious 'error' on the King's tombstone, which is marked 'Elvis Aaron Presley'. In 1997 Danna Yarmowich, described as a 'Graceland spokeswoman', revealed that Presley's middle name had originally been spelt with just one 'A' to match the single 'A' in the middle name of his stillborn twin, Jessie Garon Presley. Was this double-A inscription, then, a coded message that Elvis did not lie here beneath the sod?

This all reminded me of the Yorkshire widower who was briefing the stonemason about the inscription for his late wife's gravestone. 'Put, "She was thine",' he said, but when he returned to inspect the work he was horrified: 'You've written, "She was *thin*". You've left the "E" off.' The apologetic mason said he would correct the mistake at once, but when the bereaved man went back, he was greeted by the following inscription: 'Ee she was thin'. I think a similar thing might have happened with Elvis's memorial stone.

About the time of the gravestone theory, another claim emerged. One of the King's security men, the delightfully named Dick Grob, announced that the Mob had ordered Elvis to be 'hit' to shut him up. It seems that Presley, codename 'Fountain Pen', had been caught up in a shady FBI investigation involving organised crime and billions of dollars, and was threatening to spill the beans. Grob reckoned one of Presley's various hangers-on had let the killer into the house and, presumably, also into the toilet. The FBI had rather fallen down on protecting their agent, he felt.

The government-agent angle certainly has something to support it, as in 1970 Presley had turned up at the White House, asking to have a quick chat with President Richard Nixon, if he wasn't doing anything. Nixon's PR team sensed a young-vote-winning opportunity so an informal chat was quickly arranged and photographs taken. Nixon, it goes, later had Presley made a special drug agent, before the pop superstar pulled out by faking his own death.

A more plausible and more optimistic version of the Mob-hit scenario comes from a group of interesting people, known to themselves as 'The Presley Commission'. They allege that Presley's death and burial were simulated, and that the singer was given a new identity as part of a witness protection programme. In place of the King a wax dummy was interred, kept cool under the southern sun by discreet fans and bucketloads of dry ice. A bit like the Corpse Who Fooled Hitler (*see page 98*).

The main evidence that Elvis Presley is alive consists of hundreds of 'sightings' and a few snaps of the suitably aged 'King', some quite recent, shopping in Memphis or turning up at parties. Books and the tabloid press have churned out column-miles on this subject. In 2016, a video surfaced showing a white-bearded, shuffling, pot-bellied groundsman fiddling with a hose at Graceland. This is said to be the ageing Presley, decked out in baseball cap and ill-fitting jeans, who, it is claimed, gives a secret sign. I quote: 'He raises his 2 fingers to *the top of his left head* as a proof-of-life signal.' All I can say is that, when I looked, this man only seemed to have *one* head.

Perhaps the most interesting, even charming, Elvis conspiracy theory emerged in 2009. This claims that Michael Jackson and Elvis now live together in a deep bunker beneath Graceland, along with some other 'dead' celebrities. No worries, then, whether the pair are lonesome tonight. It's rather sweet, isn't it?

Paul McCartney Is Dead

Sometime around 1967, an enigmatic listener rang in to an American radio show and asked the DJ to play something from the Beatles' new *White Album*. He suggested the beginning of the track 'Revolution 9', but played *backwards*. The hidden message revealed by listening to this piece in reverse was to light the fuse that would ignite the most enduring conspiracy theory in the history of modern music.

Broadcast in reverse, the incriminating crystal-clear admission of a guilty conscience was revealed to listeners in the message 'Turn me on, dead man' in the bit containing the words 'Number nine'. To be honest, when I had a little backwards listen on my computer, 'Turn me on, dead man' sounded more like 'Any yarn, dudman?': a bit like someone asking the aggregate company of that name if they had any spare wool. While I was about it, I stumbled upon a man called Roger Ordish saying 'We won, now you' into a tape recorder and then playing it backwards. What comes out is, 'We won, now you.' You should try it some time.

This was a slow fuse, but after an article headed 'Is Beatle Paul McCartney Dead?' appeared in an American student newspaper, the rocket took off in a blaze of glory. The dramatic story went this way. On 7 January 1966 (other sources have 9 November), the Beatles were recording together when a flaming argument burst out and McCartney left in a huff, and in his car. As he drove along the dark, newly built M1 the distracted musician crashed and was decapitated. Then, possibly at the behest of MI5, or maybe of their own accord, the remaining Beatles decided to pull a switcheroo and swapped Paul with a Scots orphan named William Shears Campbell (later known as Billy Shears), who was the winner of a Paul McCartney lookalike contest. The band hoped this would fend off the weeping and wailing and gnashing of teeth that McCartney's death would undoubtedly cause among fans. After training their clone to impersonate Paul, the band left guilt-stricken secret messages in their songs, and in the pictures on their album covers. These hidden clues referred obliquely to Paul's death and reincarnation.

Anyway, there was now a lust among fans to play Beatles records backwards in the hope of finding more clues, and it wasn't long before secret-message-hunting truffle pigs snuffled out an abundance of succulent morsels. For example, the *Sgt. Pepper's Lonely Hearts Club Band* album features John Lennon's song 'A Day in the Life', in which the words 'Paul is dead, miss him, miss him' rang out like a klaxon, but only from tape machines going backwards. Some reverse-listeners also claimed that 'Strawberry Fields Forever' (recorded at the end of 1966) finished with John saying, 'I buried Paul'. Talk about hiding in plain sight.

Excited fans now began examining Beatles album covers under the microscope in the search for more hidden messages. The cover of *Yesterday and Today* (1966) showed the Beatles dressed as butchers, with joints of meat and decapitated dolls on their laps. This was said to be a clear reference to McCartney's motorway head-removal. With the *Sgt. Pepper* album cover, fans used a mirror to horizontally bisect the words *Lonely Hearts* on the drum, revealing the hidden message 'I ONE IX HE DIE', which was said to represent the day of Paul's death (9 November). Fans who examined the *Abbey Road* cover, showing the three remaining Beatles (and the clone) crossing the road, realised it was clearly a funeral procession, with a white-clad vicar (John), the mourner (Ringo) in black garb and the gravedigger (George) in jeans. The Paul lookalike was barefoot, for why would you need shoes when you're dead? What's more, he was walking out of step with the others, right foot forward. That clinched it. The only thing is that, when I checked other shots from the photoshoot for this album cover, I found that some show Paul wearing sandals, and in others he is not out of step with his friends.

Also in the cover picture, nonchalantly parked behind the four musicians, is a white Volkswagen Beetle. Its number plate is LMW 28IF. It was claimed that '28IF' stood for Paul's age (28) *if* he had still been alive, and 'LMW' stood for 'Linda McCartney, Widow', which is obvious when you think about it, though I suppose it could equally have meant 'Lennon McCartney: Wealthy'.

Contrary to fears, there was no grief at these discoveries. People seemed to like the 'clone Paul' as much as the 'real Paul'. But what did the man himself think of it all? McCartney remarked that when he got a call telling him he was dead, he said, 'Oh, I don't agree with that,' and, being the businessman he is, added that it would 'probably be the best publicity we've ever had and I won't have to do a thing except stay alive'. He was right: after the conspiracy theory became well known, Capitol Records reported a significant sales boost of Beatles albums. *Sgt. Pepper* and *Magical Mystery Tour* re-entered the *Billboard* Top LPs chart, and *Abbey Road* outsold all of the band's previous albums.

By the autumn of 1969, several records from other artists had been released, cashing in on the story. These included 'Brother Paul' by somebody calling himself Billy Shears and 'So Long, Paul' by the exquisitely named Werbley Finster.

Throughout the long life of this quirky conspiracy theory, the Beatles' press office continued to deny the rumour, politely calling it 'a load of old rubbish'. The Beatles too poured cold water on the idea. John Lennon said that in 'Strawberry Fields Forever', the words people had heard as 'I buried Paul' were actually 'Cranberry sauce', and Ringo Starr remarked: 'If people are gonna believe it, they're gonna believe it. I can only say it's not true.'

The Paul-McCartney-is-a-clone conspiracy theory is only one of a number of recurring reincarnation stories that go back to the Bible and to the oral traditions of

other ancient religions. Fairy tales too are full of trans-
formations like this: the frog who becomes a prince, the
beast who becomes Beauty's human suitor. These are
stories about human change, and change, after all, is the
essence of all good stories.

But if the changed figure is identical to the real McCoy,
and the impostor's wife and friends can't tell the difference, who cares? All you can say, I suppose, is that
whether it was Paul McCartney or his lookalike who
married Heather Mills and then went through a gruesome divorce, the experience was probably enough to
make the poor fellow *wish* he was dead.

IV

LIGHTING THE FUSE

Historical Conspiracies

If you would be a real seeker after truth,
it is necessary that at least once in your
life you doubt, as far as possible,
all things.

—RENÉ DESCARTES

The Gunpowder Plot

The Gunpowder Plot was an early-seventeenth-century assassination plan by a band of English Catholics. By blowing up the House of Lords during the State Opening of Parliament, on 5 November 1605, the conspirators hoped to do away with the Protestant King James I and his government and restore a Catholic monarch. The plot was scuppered at the last moment.

The conspirators, who included Guy Fawkes – a chap with a fantastic hat and a pointy beard – were led by Robert Catesby: similar hat and beard. To prepare the explosion Catesby's gang rented a cellar beneath the House of Lords – security was a bit lax back then – where they stashed thirty-six barrels of gunpowder, plenty enough to blow the place to smithereens. The man put in charge of the barrels was Guy Fawkes.

But there was trouble afoot. William Parker, 4th Baron Monteagle, had received an anonymous letter warning him of the danger. He alerted the authorities and the cellars were searched on the evening of 4 November. There the king's men found Guy Fawkes, skulking near the explosive barrels. He was arrested and over the next few days questioned under torture. He confessed to the plot, and named names, dropping his chums right in it.

His fleeing co-conspirators were chased to Holbeche House, a hundred miles north of London, in what is now the West Midlands, where they holed up. While they were there, their store of gunpowder was rained on so they decided to dry it out in front of the fire. This was tactical thinking of a rather low order, because, as they sat waiting for it to dry, a spark seems to have set it off, causing a fire that killed some of the group and probably attracted the attention of most of Staffordshire. The rest either fled or were caught the next day, when the house was surrounded by the Sheriff of Worcester and his men. Here a doubtless dazed Catesby, with what might now have been a rather singed beard, was shot and killed. Holbeche House is now a nursing home, and though much of the original building was destroyed, bullet marks can still be seen in what remain of the original walls.

In the end the Gunpowder Plot nearly worked, but Guy Fawkes, along with several fellow conspirators, was finally taken to trial on 27 January 1606. Eight of the survivors, including Fawkes, were convicted of high treason, the punishment for which was to be hanged, drawn and quartered. The attorney general told the court that Fawkes would be dragged backwards by a horse, his head near the ground. He would then be hanged by the neck until nearly dead but still semiconscious. His genitals would be cut off and burnt in front of him, before his innards were cut out and thrown onto the fire while he watched. After that his heart would be torn out and his head chopped off, which was probably a bit of a relief. Finally, his body would be sawn into quarters to be hung out as 'prey for the fowls of the air', with no chance of parole.

Bad though this was for Fawkes, it might also have been utterly unfair, because, conspiracy upon conspiracy, a recent theory suggests that although Britain's most famous terrorist was apparently at the heart of this plot to murder King James I, he was, in fact, secretly working for the monarch.

It is claimed that the king was well aware of the Gunpowder Plot and, for maximum political capital, waited until the last moment before ordering a search of the cellars. Other conspiracy theorists go further, saying that James's government used agent provocateurs to nudge the conspirators this way and that. Guy Fawkes, they claim, was just the patsy (*see* 'The Assassination of John F. Kennedy', *page 18*). A related theory suggests that agents of the Crown were acting to inflame anti-Catholic feeling so as to justify the introduction of repressive laws, and boost support for the monarch. Further evidence for Crown involvement in the Plot is said to be that in 1605 only the state had access to gunpowder in the amounts needed to blow up the House of Lords.

But, whatever the truth, Guy Fawkes got his own back. On 31 January 1606, as he was staggering up the ladder to be hanged, Fawkes fell or leapt from the scaffold and broke his neck. Despite his lowly foot-soldier status, he was to become the face of the Gunpowder Plot. A stylised smiling Guy Fawkes face with red cheeks, moustache and pointy beard became a protestor's must-have after it appeared as an illustration by David Lloyd in *V for Vendetta*, Alan Moore's British graphic story (1982–1989). This image of Fawkes duly became a symbol, and a handy mask, for the online 'hacktivist' group Anonymous and other anti-establishment groups.

For many years the thwarting of the Gunpowder Plot was commemorated in England by sermons and the ringing of church bells, celebrations that evolved into the Bonfire Night of modern times, when the supposed traitor's effigy is commonly burned on a bonfire, accompanied by fireworks, fried sausages and long queues at A&E.

The Pyramids of Ancient Egypt

I can only remember two of the Seven Wonders of the World. One is the Hanging Gardens of Babylon, which my grandma used to call the hanging *baskets* of Babylon. The other is the only one of the Seven Wonders still remaining: the Great Pyramid of Giza. Also known as the Pyramid of Cheops, the Great Pyramid stands on the west bank of the Egyptian Nile. It is part of a group of three built as royal tombs by the Ancient Egyptians and finished in about 2560 BCE. For 4,000 years it was the tallest man-made structure in the world, until they put the top on Lincoln Cathedral.

The square footprint of the Great Pyramid covers an area about the size of Windsor Castle. It is made of an estimated two million stone blocks, each weighing anything from two tons (twenty baby elephants) to thirty tons (four or five big ones). All the pyramids were constructed without sophisticated tools. The sloping sides were built as steps and the 'gaps' filled in afterwards with limestone, to leave a smooth slope. To prevent theft of their many treasures, the pyramids contain narrow corridors and secret chambers. Most of their loot is, however, thought to have been pinched within a couple of hundred years of their being finished, presumably by very skinny thieves.

These wonderful structures, the pyramids, tell us so much about the human ingenuity, physical prowess, inventiveness and mathematical acumen of the ancients. What's more, there is something compelling about their mystery, which has fertilised endless conspiracy theories that claim they were not really built by the Egyptians – or not in any normal way. As well as alien-invader theories there are Illuminati-pyramid theories, lost-civilisation pyramid theories, levitation-building-methods theories, biblical-connection theories and even a notion that the pyramids align with the three stars in Orion's Belt.

John Taylor's 1859 book *The Great Pyramid: Why It Was Built and Who Built It* sets out a mathematical theory. He had never seen the Pyramid of Giza but had got all interested anyway. He claimed it was built using the 'pyramid inch', which was nearly, but not quite, identical to the 'British inch', and that by dividing the height of the pyramid by twice the length of its base – I think that's what he meant – you get something rather like pi. Taylor felt all this was significant, and was convinced that Noah had built the Great Pyramid. This wasn't really a conspiracy theory, but it showed the sort of ideas that fans of these enigmatic structures could conjure up.

In 1882 Ignatius Loyola Donnelly (1831–1901), a sometime Minnesota Congressman and fringe theorist with ideas about Atlantis, Catastrophism and Shakespearean authorship (*see page 85*), claimed that the Atlanteans established a colony in Egypt and had a hand in the building of the pyramids. American clairvoyant Edgar Cayce (1877–1945), dubbed the 'Sleeping Psychic', agreed with Donnelly on the Atlantis business, while in a self-induced 'sleep state'. He was author of the interesting idea that there were five human races – White, Black, Red, Brown and Yellow – and believed the pyramids to have been built by a conspiratorial consortium of Russian Whites, Egyptian Browns and Atlanteans of some indeterminate hue, who used their combined mental powers to lift the stones into place.

In the twentieth century science came to the fore in the search for answers to the pyramids' mysterious powers. During the fifties you could get yourself a 'Cheops Razorblade Sharpener', basically just a cardboard pyramid that you put over your blades. The pyramid razorblade sharpener boomed briefly but didn't last because, it was rumoured, the giant razorblade companies didn't like the look of what an endlessly sharp blade would do to their share price.

The pyramid-power idea took off in the seventies, when a proliferation of home-friendly pyramids were advertised. These did not claim to sharpen your razor but did practically everything else, from ageing wine to improving television reception.

One theory says that Egyptian official investigators have recently found in the Great Pyramid evidence of a lost civilisation, which they are keeping to themselves. Officials have gone as far as to admit that robots roaming some ventilation shafts running from the 'Queen's Chamber' found what looked like doors with handles.

They made a hole in the first of these doors and pushed in a small camera, revealing another door hidden behind the first, at which point nobody would say any more. What was it they were trying to hide behind that second door? The secret lay, some said, in the essence of the pyramid itself, which for centuries has been a symbol of the Illuminati (*see page 187*).

The Eye of Horus is visible on many Ancient Egyptian finds, and is often depicted on pyramids. Horus was the Ancient Egyptian's sky god, usually depicted as a falcon-headed man, and his distinctive eye was a symbol of protection and royal power. As one of the emblems of the Illuminati it has become known as the All-seeing Eye. Often it appears surrounded by sun rays. It is prominent on the floating tip of the pyramid on the reverse of the US dollar bill, and, though officially said to be the protective eye of God, some say it represents the baleful gaze of the Illuminati (*see page 187*), or the Masons, and their friends in the military-industrial complex.

That is all very well, but what we did not know until recently is how the Egyptian builders, under the power of the All-seeing Eye, decided where to place them. In their 1994 book *The Orion Mystery* (easily confused with *The Onion Mystery* if you haven't got your glasses on), Robert Bauval and Adrian Gilbert claimed that the pyramids were really built 12,000 years ago, and used photographs to show the relationship between their positioning and the stars that appear in the belt of the constellation Orion.

Inspecting this theory, the director of the Griffith Observatory in Los Angeles, Ed Krupp, noticed something interesting about Bauval and Gilbert's images. 'The picture of the pyramids,' he said, 'is oriented with north at the bottom of the page. Orion's Belt, on the other hand, has north at the top. To make the pyramids match the sky, you have to turn Egypt upside-down.' Could Egypt have been turned upside-down 12,000 years ago? It seems unlikely, but who knows what the mental powers of the Atlanteans and those ingenious Browns might have accomplished?

The Knights Templar

The monastic order of the Knights Templar was one of many created after the sizzling success of the First Crusade (1096–1099). The Crusades were a series of medieval religious wars that aimed to take from Islamic rule land that is now Turkey, Syria, Lebanon, Israel and Jordan – juicy pies into which the fingers of Christian countries are still stuck. To protect them from angry members of the Eastern Orthodox Church, Muslims and bandits, the Crusaders asked the Pope to establish a fighting monastic order. He did, and the Knights Templar were born. They chose as their HQ Jerusalem's Temple Mount, the site hallowed in Judaism, Christianity and Islam alike. It was the reputed location of Solomon's Temple and home to the Ark of the Covenant, the chest containing the original stone tablets on which were inscribed the Ten Commandments. With the temple as their base the choice of the order's name couldn't have been more obvious: the Knights Templar.

In their stylish uniform of white mantle with red cross the Templars were known as the Crusade's finest warriors. Membership grew rapidly, though some 90 per cent were non-fighting, and for about the next two hundred years the institution of the Knights Templar was one of the world's most powerful, effectively the first multinational corporation and an early form of global bank. The Templars were funded at first by charitable patrons but after a time their successful investments and lending allowed them to fund themselves.

By 1307, however, King Philip IV of France, deeply in debt to the order, wanted rid of the Knights Templar. Secular powers too were becoming jumpy, and suspicious of their sway. As with the Freemasons, whispers about the Templars' secret initiation rites began to ruffle feathers and, spotting his chance, the king had a word with Pope Clement V, who quickly wound up the order in 1312. Naturally, the sudden fading of this potent European secret society soon led to claims of conspiracy and rumours that its members had gone underground.

One mysterious theory alleges that the Knights Templar had reached the New World two hundred years before Columbus, leaving treasures in the Oak Island money pit in Nova Scotia. These included the Ark of the Covenant, or possibly the Holy Grail, the cup said to have been used by Jesus at the Last Supper. Unfortunately, though eager beavers have been digging since 1795, not much has been dug up apart from some old bits of wood and a gold-plated button dropped by a nineteenth-century treasure hunter. There was some excitement when a Roman-era bronze sword was unearthed, but this turned out to be a brass gift-shop gewgaw from the 1970s.

Various elements of the Knights Templar story crop up in books such as *The Da Vinci Code* (2003), and films like *Indiana Jones and the Last Crusade* (1989), and it might be that this began with a conspiracy theory that appeared in the 1982 book *Holy Blood, Holy Grail* by Michael Baigent, Richard Leigh and Henry Lincoln.

This theory purports to expose the truth of the Holy Grail: that it is not only a cup, but also a term referring at once to Mary Magdalene's womb and the bloodline that she began. The true story apparently goes this way: Jesus's death was faked and he married Mary Magdalene, one of the witnesses at his 'crucifixion'. Their child, or children, or possibly their descendants, moved to what is now the bottom bit of France, where they married members of the aristocracy and conquered much of Gaul, eventually becoming the Merovingian dynasty, known as the 'long-haired kings', owing to the luscious locks that marked them out from the buzz-cut Germanic Franks, whom they ruled. It is said they were the progenitors of every European royal family, and that a secret society called the Priory of Sion today pushes their supposed claim to the French throne. The ultimate aim of all this is a pan-European government led by the present head of the House of Habsburg.

Reviewing *Holy Blood, Holy Grail* in 1982, novelist and lapsed Catholic Anthony Burgess called it 'a marvellous theme for a novel', and Dan Brown's 2003 book *The Da Vinci Code* does seem to borrow some of its concepts. The Roman Catholic Church had other ideas, and in some countries banned *Holy Blood, Holy Grail* as blasphemous, thus boosting its sales enormously, though there are also claims that the Church has always been aware of the true Mary Magdalene bloodline story and is involved in hushing it all up.

Critics of the various conspiracy theories surrounding the Knights Templar argue that most of them are 'pseudo-historical'. The trouble with this accusation is that similar claims can be made about the Bible itself. By the same token, much generally accepted history is also open to doubt. Even accounts of living-memory events such as the Watergate burglary (*see page 165*) and 9/11 (*see page 153*) are said to be full of holes. The makers of history themselves cannot be relied on. For example, numerous solemn promises given after prayers in the House of Commons have turned out to be false, from Mr Profumo forgetting he'd been to bed with a woman who wasn't his wife, to the cash-for-questions and parliamentary expenses scandals.

The Church got quite upset about the claimed religious practices of the Templars, who were said to have worshipped not Jesus, but John the Baptist. As part of their seven-hundred-year-old secret rituals it is claimed they spat on a crucifix and venerated a mysterious decapitated head. As if it weren't difficult enough to get to the bottom of academically rigorous conspiracy theories, the internal inconsistencies in some of them can make the serious researcher's job almost impossible.

The confusion was brought up to date in July 2012, when Norwegian far-right terrorist Anders Behring Breivik killed eight people by detonating a van bomb in Oslo, before shooting dead sixty-nine members of a summer camp on the island of Utøya. Having once photographed himself in homemade 'Knights Templar' get-up, with fake medals and badges, Breivik claimed to be a member of what he called the 'reborn Knights Templar', a 'terrorist organisation' he had apparently created from details in the computer game *World of Warcraft*. Unlike the Crusaders of old, however, his 'reborn Knights Templar' seem to have existed only in his own head. It all looked like a childish fantasy, a simplified view of a complicated world, but one which led to irredeemably tragic results.

The Shakespeare Conspiracy

In 1845, two hundred and twenty-nine years after the death of William Shakespeare (1564–1616), American critic Delia Bacon began suggesting that he had not written his plays, but that they had been done by a group of literary conspirators guided by Sir Francis Bacon – the English philosopher and statesman, not the painter of screaming popes, and no relation to Delia, as far as I know. This literary gang, Delia suggested, included Edmund Spenser, Lord Buckhurst and Edward de Vere, 17th Earl of Oxford. Sir Walter Raleigh, she reckoned, was the principal author.

Three years later, as frequently happens after a lone voice has suggested a provocative conspiracy theory, another person popped up with similar ideas, this time in a book. Joseph C. Hart was the chap, and his title was, surprisingly, *The Romance of Yachting* (1848), in which he elaborated, in passing, on the Shakespearean authorship question. Four years later *Chambers's Edinburgh Journal* published an essay entitled 'Who Wrote Shakespeare?' outlining similar ideas. The author was anonymous and people asked themselves, 'Who wrote "Who Wrote Shakespeare?"?' Though Delia Bacon had started the ball rolling, her own book on the subject did not appear until the following decade.

Very little is known about William Shakespeare's life, which has led to speculation, some fairly wild, about his looks, religion, genital attributes, sexual proclivities and whether he wrote his own plays. We know he was born in 1564, in a pleasant house in Stratford-upon-Avon. He went to the local school and married a local girl, Ann Hathaway, with whom he had three children, including a boy called Hamnet, not Hamlet. He had a successful career in London as an actor, writer and part-owner of a theatrical company, retiring to Stratford aged forty-nine, where he died, on his birthday, in 1616.

The American humorist Mark Twain was a great proponent of the idea that William Shakespeare never wrote any of the plays attributed to him and was but a mere businessman. 'Shakespeare didn't know he was a writer,' said Twain, 'and nobody told him until after he was dead.' 'So far as anybody knows and can prove, Shakespeare of Stratford-on-Avon wrote only one poem during his life ... He commanded that this work of art be engraved upon his tomb. There it abides to this day. This is it:'

Good frend for Jesus Sake forbeare,
To digg the dust encloased heare.
Blese be ye man yt spares thes stones
And curst be he yt moves my bones.

Most people agree this is appalling doggerel; it's almost as bad as the famous 'Underneath this pile of stones / Is all that's left of Sally Jones. / Her name was Smith, it wasn't Jones, / But "stones" was used to rhyme with "Jones"'. Still, as they remarked of Ophelia when she said 'there is pansies', she wasn't herself at the time.

It is generally acknowledged that in the last part of his life, William Shakespeare did collaborate with other playwrights. For example, *The Two Noble Kinsmen*, now considered Shakespeare's final play, was written with playwright John Fletcher. But in 2016 scholars working on Oxford's Shakespeare collection went further. Using 'textual analysis' and 'computerised tools' to examine the scripts of all his known works, they concluded that seventeen out of forty-four plays they looked at were co-written with other authors, and identified the 'presence' of Christopher Marlowe 'strongly and clearly' in three. It had first been suggested in the eighteenth century that Marlowe and Shakespeare had written together, but a collaboration is not a conspiracy, and, in any case, other experts disagreed.

Those who do not believe Shakespeare wrote *any* of his own plays are called 'Anti-Stratfordians', a useful term that covers a multitude of different conspiracy theories about who the true author was. Some say that Mr Shakespeare, the Man from Stratford, was just a front who allowed the real authors to write all those plays and poems. Several reasons for the true authors' literary bashfulness have been put forward, including his being of too low or too high a social rank, being the wrong sex and even national security. The alleged authors now number eighty or more, with Bacon in the lead, the Earls of Oxford and Derby close behind, and Christopher Marlowe bringing up the rear.

William Shakespeare left six signatures, and all are different in their spelling. This is regarded by some as clear evidence they were the work of self-confident impostors who didn't even bother to get the name right. The variant spellings are: *Willm Shakp*; *William Shaksper*; *Wm Shakspe*; *William Shakspere*; *Willm Shakspere* and *By me William Shakspeare*. However, it must be remembered that standardised pronunciation and firm spelling conventions did not become settled in England until centuries after Shakespeare's time. Even today you have to use your judgment/judgement when ordering a scone/scon.

The 'other-people-wrote-it-all' theorists say there isn't a single slip of paper that identifies Shakespeare as a writer. He is described on documents as a businessman with financial interests in the theatre. There's that, plus a bit of acting. But one mustn't mistake absence of evidence for evidence of absence. It is true that we know almost nothing of the man's life, but that is the same with many playwrights of the time.

Few people ever disagree about the genius of whoever it was who authored these plays and poems, but some have suggested that, as the son of a humble glove-maker, with a largely unrecorded life, William Shakespeare didn't have what it took to produce such great poetic and dramatic masterpieces. This is sheer social snobbery of the sort you might read in the Sunday newspapers or hear on arts programmes on the radio. And to think that poor Willm Shakp lay unmolested in his grave for centuries, his artistic reputation and social standing unblemished, till these nineteenth-century 'literary critics' crawled out of the woodwork.

Shakespeare's authorship of his own work went unquestioned while he was alive, and for centuries after he died, and in the end, as so often, the obvious conclusion is the obvious conclusion. Shakespeare was a man, he was writer, and, like Anton Chekhov or Thomas Hardy, he was especially good at what he did. There is evidence for all this. It comes from the stylistic consistency of the plays and poems, the plays' title pages, the testament of contemporaneous historians, and from the accolades his poet and playwright colleagues gave him at the time. There's nothing half as good as this for any of the proposed conspirators being the true author.

V

ON THE WARPATH

Military Conspiracies

Nothing is more easy than to
deceive one's self.

—DEMOSTHENES

Weather Control

On 15 August 1952, Britain recorded one of its worst ever flash floods, when a massive deluge of water, and thousands of tons of rock, poured off the already-soaked Exmoor hills into the Devon village of Lynmouth. The term 'flash flood' describes rapid inundation caused by very heavy rain falling onto saturated or unabsorbent ground. With nowhere to go this water runs off, often creating fast-flowing streams of debris.

Even before the Lynmouth rainstorm, the River Lyn, which flows through the village, had become choked with fallen trees and debris, forming a dam, which finally gave way. This sent a huge wave roaring through the streets, demolishing or damaging more than a hundred buildings and twenty-eight of the village's thirty-one bridges. About forty cars were washed out to sea, thirty-four people died, and more than four hundred were rendered homeless.

Heavy rain is quite normal and flash flooding is a predictable event, but previously classified government files appear to suggest that in August 1952 an international team of scientists were working with the RAF near Lynmouth on a procedure known as 'cloud seeding', and that this exploratory weather modification might have been implicated in the great flood.

In cloud seeding, particles of dry ice or silver iodide are released into clouds, causing condensation of water vapour or ice nuclei. This results in 'artificial' rain or snow over a distance of up to 300 miles. Military reasons for the technique include increasing flooding and river-flow to bog down enemy troops and hinder their movement. In one recorded US weather-control manoeuvre, called 'Operation Popeye', clouds were seeded to extend the Vietnam monsoon. More drastic measures include exploding atomic weapons in seeded systems to produce a much wider area of radioactive contamination than usual. Weather modification during warfare is now forbidden by the United Nations.

Although the Ministry of Defence denied knowledge of any UK cloud-seeding experiments during early August 1952, a BBC documentary described how previously classified government documents suggested a cloud-seeding scheme known as Operation Cumulus was indeed under way between 4 August and 15 August. Scientists from Cranfield College of Aeronautics were, it seems, working with the RAF and the MoD at Farnborough, the chemicals being supplied by ICI. BBC Radio found supporting evidence in RAF logbooks. Aeronautical engineer Alan Yates, who had seeded clouds during Operation Cumulus, said he had been delighted when his actions led to rain. 'I was told that the rain had been the heaviest for several years,' he explained, 'and all out of a sky which looked summery …' Another cloudseeder, Group Captain John Hart, remembered flying straight through the top of a cloud, pouring dry ice down into it and seeing rain emerge about half an hour later. 'We all cheered,' he told the BBC.

Some survivors of the Lynmouth flood described a strange smell in the air that afternoon and said the rain fell so hard it hurt their faces. Others demanded a full investigation, but, though Operation Cumulus was suspended indefinitely, no inquiry was forthcoming. Rumours of planes circling overhead before the flood are said to persist, and silver residue has been discovered in the catchment waters of the River Lyn.

Cloud seeding is part of a bigger programme of weather control, sometimes also termed 'weather modification' or 'climate engineering', which has been a favourite conspiracy theory for decades.

All the same, sceptical weatherman Philip Eden, vice president of the Royal Meteorological Society from 2007 to 2009, said it was 'preposterous' to blame the Lynmouth flood on such experiments. The storm was not confined to Lynmouth, and, in any case, similar disastrous floods had occurred in the village in 1607 and 1796.

In 2018, 222 years later, a very weird giant 'square cloud' with impossible crisp ninety-degree corners was filmed in the sky in Tucson, Arizona. You can find photographs of similar square clouds on the internet. These deeply strange pictures have led to claims that a US government radio-technology programme, known as 'HAARP' (High-frequency Active Auroral Research Program), was responsible. HAARP was designed to analyse the ionosphere so as to improve radio communication and surveillance, but some say it is a top-secret US 'weather-weaponising' project, the cause not only of cloud anomalies, but also Hurricane Katrina, in 2005, and sundry earthquakes and tsunamis. Theorists have concluded that the government is 'trying to manipulate the elements', but whether that means controlling the weather or using a computer to fake the images of square clouds is a good question. Nowadays even a teenager lurking in his bedroom with a laptop and a bit of software can produce miracles of this sort.

HAARP has also been blamed for chemically altering aeroplane vapour trails to change the weather: the so-called 'chemtrail conspiracy theory'. However, a study examining temperatures during the shutdown of civil air traffic following 9/11 (*see page 153*) showed that aeroplane vapour trails and 'contrail-induced cirrus clouds' contribute only weakly to temperature changes during daytime, which are controlled mainly by clouds, wind and humidity nearer the ground. The weather when there were no vapour trails stayed much the same as before, as it did during the longer COVID-19 air-traffic shutdown.

US President Donald Trump was very interested not only in conspiracy theories, but also in weather control. News website Axios reported that Trump had wondered in a meeting with security officials whether the US military shouldn't destroy hurricanes by bombing them before they hit the USA. 'I got it. I got it,' he was quoted as saying. 'Why don't we nuke them? ... They start forming off the coast of Africa, as they're moving across the

Atlantic, we drop a bomb inside the eye of the hurricane and it disrupts it. Why can't we do that?' The National Oceanic and Atmospheric Administration remarked, 'Needless to say, this is not a good idea,' and MIT hurricane expert Kerry Emanuel commented: 'If we have a leader who would contemplate using a nuclear weapon on a hurricane, we have a much more extensive and serious problem …' Trump had a comment of his own on the report. 'I never said this. Just more FAKE NEWS!' – his capital letters underlying the truth of his assertion.

The Corpse Who Fooled Hitler

One of the best ever military conspiracies was devised by British Intelligence during the Second World War. It was a plot that harmed nobody and possibly saved many thousands of lives. Which only goes to show that conspiracies don't have to be dark and vicious. In fact, they can sometimes be faintly ludicrous.

In late 1942, the Allies were planning a strategic invasion of Sicily. The trouble was that, as Winston Churchill put it, 'Everyone but a bloody fool would know that it's Sicily.' The Axis powers were no fools and what was needed was a fake plan that would get the Germans to take their men and weapons out of Sicily and put them somewhere completely useless.

British intelligence man RAF Flight-Lieutenant Charles Cholmondeley (pronounced *chumly*) had just such a wheeze up his sleeve: with a bunch of fake papers the British would trick the Nazis into turning their attention away from Sicily by making them think they had stumbled upon documents setting out Allied plans to invade somewhere else instead. Royal Navy intelligence officer Lieutenant-Commander Ewen Montagu developed the idea with Cholmondeley. The plan was to create some fake letters full of disinformation and put them in a brief-case attached to the body of a dead man who had apparently been in a plane crash at sea. The body would be released by a submarine off the coast of Huelva, in southwest Spain, where the tides were likely to wash it ashore. Spanish Nazi agents would then pass the documents over to the Germans.

The plan was given the deliciously British code name 'Operation Mincemeat'. Not being what it sounds – neither minced, nor meat – 'mincemeat' was the ideal word for this devious plot. It also hinted at the hoped-for effect: making mincemeat of the Germans' defences.

So, a suitable cadaver was found. It was that of thirty-four-year-old Glyndwr Michael, a lonely Welsh vagrant who had swallowed rat poison and died at St Pancras Hospital. Montagu created a new identity for the dead man, making him Captain (Acting Major) William Martin, Royal Marines. Born, so his papers said, in 1907, he was, therefore, a couple of years older than his own corpse.

Into Major Martin's uniform pockets went a bunch of keys, a letter from his father, theatre ticket stubs, and other flotsam indicating a life beyond work. There was a photograph of his fiancée, 'Pam' (actually an MI5 girl named Jean Leslie), together with two of her love letters. There were several bills, most notably one for an engage-ment ring, and a terse letter from the manager of Lloyds Bank, referring to Major Martin's overdraft.

Two carefully faked personal letters now went into his briefcase. One was addressed to Sir Harold Alexander, commander of the 18th Army Group in Algeria and Tunisia, from Lieutenant General Sir Archibald Nye, Vice Chief of the Imperial General Staff. This referred misleadingly to Operation Husky (the planned invasion of Sicily) as the invasion of *Greece*, and to an intended attack on Sardinia, for which the cover target was Sicily. There was also a letter to the Allied naval commander in the Mediterranean, from Admiral of the Fleet Earl Mountbatten, containing a joke about 'sardines', a supposed reference to the fake Sardinian invasion.

So, with the documents inside the bag, and Major Martin's pockets full of personal bits and bobs, the body was slid from the fridge, given a military haircut and dressed. The major was then sealed inside a steel canister of dry ice.

The gruesome cargo was driven overnight to Scotland, where it was put aboard a submarine, HMS *Seraph*, at Holy Loch. She set sail on 19 April, her commander telling his men that the strange container held weather forecasting equipment.

Eleven days later, the sub surfaced a mile off Huelva. The commander briefed his officers as to the true purpose of the canister and they opened it. The vital briefcase was looped around the belt of the corpse's trench coat, and the lifejacketed body was floated off into the current.

The next morning a local fisherman found the body washed up on the beach and a few days later the corpse and the briefcase, with its seemingly unopened letters, were handed over to the British vice-consul. On 4 May

'Major Martin' was buried in Huelva with full military honours.

Realising its importance, the Spanish had quickly reported their find to a local German agent, before turning their attention to the contents of the briefcase. They removed the letters from their wax-sealed envelopes by inserting a long double-pronged pincer, winding them around it, and pulling them out through the gap at the top. The letters were dried and the Germans given an hour to make copies. The nature of their contents was then radioed to Berlin. They had been hooked.

The Spanish painstakingly returned the letters to their envelopes, and soaked them in seawater, before handing them over to the British. When British intelligence examined them, they found that they had been opened. Winston Churchill received a cryptic message, 'Mincemeat swallowed whole.'

The letters got as far as Hitler, and, convinced they were legitimate, the Germans diverted military forces from Sicily into Greece, Sardinia and Corsica, allowing the Allies a much easier time of it when they invaded Sicily on 9 July.

By a combination of careful planning, good old British conspiratorial deviousness and much good luck, Operation Mincemeat had been a triumph. But for recognition of his role in this great success Glyndwr Michael had to wait. It was not until 1996, more than half a century after the event, that historian Roger Morgan uncovered the dead man's true identity; and in January 1998 the Commonwealth War Graves Commission quietly appended an inscription to the gravestone of 'Major Martin' at his burial place in Huelva. It reads simply, 'GLYNDWR MICHAEL SERVED AS MAJOR WILLIAM MARTIN, RM'.

Stench Soup and the Gay Bomb

It is well known that governments and the military conduct research into deadly weapons and conspire to keep all this a secret not just from the enemy, but from us voters, the poor suckers who pay for it all. Sometimes this research is odd.

At the time of the Pearl Harbor attack, dentist Dr Lytle Adams had just returned from New Mexico, where he had been 'tremendously impressed' by cave-dwelling free-tailed bats. Realising they were ideal for coaching as bomb-carrying secret weapons, he set out a plan to obliterate Japanese cities in revenge for Pearl Harbor by training these animals to emigrate, loaded with tiny bombs. They would, he guessed, 'frighten, demoralize and excite the prejudices of the Japanese Empire', and would also, presumably, blow things up.

He forwarded his idea to President Roosevelt who passed it to his head of intelligence, writing in an explanatory note, 'This man is not a nut.' And so it began: thousands of bats were captured from their haunts across southwest America, designs for bat-size bombs were drawn up and a way of transporting the animals proposed. But after spending some $2 million on research, and doing thirty or so batty tests, the scheme was dropped in favour of an even more secret development under way in the desert sands of Los Alamos. Codenamed the 'Manhattan Project', it was the American atom-bomb programme.

For decades after the dropping of atomic bombs on two Japanese cities, their vast destructive power gave many pause for thought, and the US government, together with the military, began research into non-lethal weapons. They set up a highly secret six-year programme budgeted at millions of dollars to investigate debilitating but non-lethal weapons designed to demoralise the enemy and disrupt discipline. A secret US document titled 'Harassing, Annoying and Bad Guy Identifying Chemicals' sketched out ideas for chemical sprays for squirting onto enemy troops, to produce a variety of unusual effects.

There was a 'sting me/attack me' bomb, which would provoke swarms of furious wasps and enraged rats to set upon enemy forces, and another that would cause unbearable sun sensitivity in the skin of enemy troops. There was even a proposal for a chemical-spray bomb that would cause 'severe and lasting halitosis'. This, it was claimed, would identify those trying to infiltrate themselves into allied society, at the same time making the infiltrator highly unattractive to the wives of US and British forces. They could have saved themselves a lot of research money here and just looked back to the Second World War, when the Spanish, Italian and French used just such a weapon. It is called garlic.

The whole military conspiracy was top secret. As for the public interest in these ideas, Captain Dan McSweeney of the Joint Non-Lethal Weapons Directorate at the Pentagon poured cold water on the whole thing, saying that not a single one had been developed. Of course, we must take Captain McSweeney's word for it, and I would not suggest for a minute that he had his fingers crossed behind his back.

But despite the fine words, the military, government and science establishment have continued to conspire on non-lethal weapons development. One of these brain-waves had been kicked around since 1945: a bomb to simulate the effects of severe farting in the enemy ranks.

In 1997, in an effort to develop such a chemical, the US military approached the high priestess of pong, smell researcher Pamela Dalton. They asked her to come up with a powerfully disgusting stench that would work on every nationality and race, causing cross-cultural heaving and running away.

Dalton, who got the bit between her teeth pretty quickly, explained that it is biological odours that produce the strongest human reactions: the smell of things that are likely to make you ill, such as vomit, excrement, rotting fish, garbage and corpses, are all prime candidates for research. More recently, she was even alerted to a promising research opportunity by the friend of a person named 'Gary', who said that throwing a pair of Gary's unspeakable pants or socks into the caves of the Taliban in Afghanistan would cause the enemy to run out in confusion, hands up and eyes streaming.

Until Dalton unveiled her masterpiece of stink, which we will come to shortly, the officially smelliest substance in the world was a product called US Government Standard Bathroom Malodor, an unbelievably foul faecal reek used to challenge newly developed lavatory air fresheners. Of course, the idea that these vastly expensive super-stink research projects were for the testing of toilet deodorants was a handy cover for the military, who were providing the money. One test volunteer said the smell of Bathroom Malodor was so strong it filled his whole head.

The second smelliest product was the mild-sounding Who me? – a combination of several bad-egg chemical pongs with an afterburn of rotting food and death. This is said to be so disgusting that it caused a lot of angry multi-cultural swearing among otherwise mild-mannered test volunteers.

In her brilliance, Pamela Dalton combined these two astonishing niffs to produce Stench Soup, a world-beatingly foul fetor that causes people to swoon and want to run for their lives. Strangely, says Dalton, the most disgusting smells work best when they also contain an attractive perfume. Adding floral and fruit aromas, she revealed, made the thing 'so disgusting none of us could stand it', and she's a stink-hardened smeller.

Variety, though, is the spice of conspiracy, and in the 1990s the US Air Force came up with a variation: they decided to make love, not war. A proposal from the Air Force's Wright Laboratory in Dayton, Ohio, put it this way: 'One distasteful but non-lethal example [of a chemical-spray bomb] would be strong aphrodisiacs, especially if the chemical also caused homosexual behaviour.' Could enemy troops be sprayed with a pheromone, aphrodisiac or other catnip-like chemical that would make their comrades so sexually irresistible that they would forget their military duties and invite them out for a candle-lit dinner instead, and then back for coffee and a look at their etchings? Could they make a gay spray, a 'gay bomb'? Judging by those old TV commercials for a deodorant called Lynx, in which a callow young man causes multitudes of young ladies with improbable chests to fight over him, this would be a doddle. The tricky bit would be making those servicemen, who weren't already, gay.

The gauntlet having been flung down, the US Air Force began looking at possibilities. In a three-page document they set out their proposal for a gay bomb: an aerosol that would be sprayed over adversaries, containing 'a chemical that would cause enemy soldiers to become gay, and to have their units break down because all their soldiers became irresistibly attractive to one another'. This gay bomb came in at the low price of $7.5 million. Like many other military and government projects, voters would have wondered about the cost of all of this, if it hadn't been a state secret.

The University of California's Palm Center studies the subject of gay people in the military. Its director, Aaron Belkin, had a final thought: 'The idea that you could submit someone to some aerosol spray and change their sexual behaviour is ludicrous,' he said.

VI

UNDER THE MICROSCOPE

Science and Health Conspiracies

Don't believe everything you
read on the internet.

—JULIUS CAESAR

The Flat-Earth Conspiracy

On 22 February 2020, the Flat Earth movement lost one of its most colourful champions, 'Mad Mike' Hughes: limousine driver, inventor, self-proclaimed nutcase, daredevil and self-taught rocket scientist. Mike was a flat-Earther with a story to tell. He explained that he had always been puzzled by the world: 'After 9/11 I just started questioning things.' It wasn't long before he noticed that the round-Earth idea didn't really stand up. 'Where is the curvature where we live? I can't find it,' said Mad Mike. 'Kansas is flat, okay? I'm tellin' you, I've been there, it's *flat*.'

In 2016, Mike began fundraising for his attempt to slip the surly bonds of Earth and take pictures of it looking all flat from his homemade rocket. He raised a disappointing $310, hardly enough for the celebration champagne, but did better at a second go, when a lot of flat-Earthers chipped in. He modestly explained that the launch into the stratosphere of his steam-powered, garage-built rocket would be 'probably the most single incredible event in mankind's history'. Most single? – hardly; most singular? – possibly.

Hopes were high at the launch site in Barstow, California, as journalists licked pencils and television directors erected tripods. Then, after a lot of steam, his homemade rocket finally took off in an impressive cloud. But before you could say health and safety the landing chute deployed prematurely behind the rocket and was blasted by the huge jet of steam, like a deflated balloon. Sixty-four-year-old Mike was then ejected from the rocket at too low a height for his own parachute to open and plunged to his death. It was sad to see him go. I liked Mike in the interviews I've seen him do. He added a bit of colour to life. Not all flat-Earthers are such fun.

Flat-Earthers insist that centuries of mathematical calculations, science observations and modern photographs of our spherical planet taken from space are part of an international conspiracy to cover up the truth that the Earth is a flat disc, above which the solar system and universe hover in a sort of shallow dome, like those plastic things they used to put over the plate of buns in railway-station cafés.

The idea that the Earth is round is older than you might think: far older than the Bible and the pyramids of Ancient Egypt. The realisation that we live on a rotating sphere, hurtling pointlessly through space, half of us upside-down, appeared in the sixth century BCE, when the ancient Ionian Greek philosopher Pythagoras happened to mention it, though the idea had probably been around before this. By about 330 BCE, Aristotle, the Greek philosopher and all-round egghead, had observed that you saw different stellar constellations as you travelled further away from the equator, and inferred the Earth's spherical shape. Over the next two centuries, other Greek mathematicians and astronomers actually worked out the size of the Earth. This knowledge gradually spread beyond the Greek world and by early medieval times it was widely understood in Europe that the Earth was round, though even then the flat-Earth idea was still popular with many. By Victorian times everyone in England realised that this strange-sounding idea was true.

In spite of this, modern conjectures that the Earth is flat began cropping up. These began with an English Bible fan named Samuel Rowbotham (1816–1884), who started small by publishing a sixteen-page pamphlet on the subject. But he couldn't stop himself and before you knew it he'd done this great big 430-page book, whose title was as terse as a news headline: *Zetetic Astronomy: Earth Not a Globe*.

Rowbotham's fancies extended the central flat-Earth idea, describing the planet as a disc with its centre at the North Pole, its southern perimeter edged by an ice-wall – which we call Antarctica. Rowbotham had been prompted to his conclusions after wondering why, if the Earth was really a sphere, the long, straight ditches on the Bedford Levels did not appear to curve. Obviously, the Earth must be flat. Like others with a new idea he felt the need to tell people and started lecturing about it all over the place. When asked at a talk in Blackburn to explain why, if the Earth was flat, the hulls of ships sailing away from observers on land dropped below the horizon before their masts, he was stumped but agreed to a test of his theory. On Plymouth Hoe, Rowbotham's round-Earth opponents set up a telescope, aiming to show that owing to the Earth's curvature only the lantern of the fourteen-mile-distant Eddystone Lighthouse would be visible. Bending down and squinting through the eyepiece, he agreed, but claimed that this evidence that his belief was false was evidence that it was true.

Rowbotham was a charismatic and persuasive salesman and entrepreneur. In later years he patented a 'life-preserving cylindrical railway carriage' and promoted various medical nostrums, before moving into a vast and expensive house. After his death, however, his ideas did not survive well, fading with his memory.

It was to be seventy-two years before another English eccentric, Samuel Shenton, founded the Flat Earth Society, in 1956. Equally sure of his theories, Shenton was untroubled when new satellite pictures showed a clearly spherical Earth. 'It's easy to see how a photograph like that could fool the untrained eye,' he said.

When Shenton died in the seventies, an American, Charles K. Johnson, took over his society, claiming that, to distract people from the biblical truth of the Earth's flatness, conspirators had faked the Moon landings (*see page 116*) and, in fact, all space exploration. Scientists who claimed it was round like every other planet in the solar system were, said Johnson, 'a gang of witch-doctors, sorcerers, tellers of tales, and "Priest-Entertainers" of the common people. Science,' he went on, 'consists of a weird, way-out occult concoction of gibberish theory-theology … unrelated to the real world of … tall buildings and fast cars, airplanes and other Real and Good things in life …'

If you find yourself looking down your nose at these opinions, and those of other flat-Earthers, and are convinced the world is round, you need to ask yourself what the evidence is that makes you so sure, how good it is and how you could prove to a sceptic that your beliefs are true. Examining your own beliefs can be a disconcerting experience because you often find the reasons you have for believing something, such as that the Earth is round, are rather like your reasons for the political, moral and religious beliefs you hold; that is to say, pretty feeble.

The Moon Landings
That Never Were

One of the most enjoyable conspiracy theories of the twentieth century, which is still very much with us, is that NASA faked the Apollo Moon landings. In 2019, a study by Ipsos found that 6 per cent of those who spoke to researchers said they believed the 1969 Moon landing was false, but 11 per cent of millennials (i.e. they were not born at the time) thought it was faked. Whether this makes them more sceptical or more gullible is debatable.

The story is that no astronauts ever landed on the Moon and the whole thing was shot on a big set with actors dangling from wires being filmed in slow motion. Much is made by conspiracy theorists of supposed anomalies in the famous photographs of the astronauts playing golf and leaping high in the air on the lunar surface, which are said to show shadows falling in the wrong places, a flag ruffled by the non-existent wind, clumsy photo-montage, stage rocks with identical surfaces, obvious wires holding the actors up and even a Coke bottle rolling across the lunar surface.

In 1980, the Flat Earth Society said NASA had asked Hollywood to stage the landings based on an Arthur C.

Clarke script, which was directed by Stanley Kubrick and sponsored by Walt Disney. Kubrick replied that if this was true he had yet to be paid, and could someone please sort this out for him.

Even at the time of the Apollo 8 lunar-orbiting mission, in 1968, similar conspiracy theories were already doing the rounds, with some claiming that the fake landings were created by the US government to distract from the Vietnam War, which was growing increasingly unpopular with the public.

One of the main focuses of conspiracy theorists has always been several strange photographic anomalies, which any observer will easily spot. For example, there are bright hotspots in some photos, caused, it is said, by a huge spotlight. Neither are there any stars in photographs, apparently because the pictures were taken on an earthly film set, not on the Moon.

The finger has also been pointed at the Apollo camera lenses, which had very fine crosshairs, for measurements to be taken when the pictures were developed. In some photos, these crosshairs seem to be *behind* objects, which must, it is claimed, have been pasted over the photographs.

Conspiracy theorists have also pointed out that some pictures captioned as being miles apart have identical backgrounds. They claim a painted backdrop was used. An Australian woman named Una Ronald went further, saying she had stayed up in the darkness to watch the Moon landing live and saw a Coca-Cola bottle roll across the corner of her TV screen. The *West Australian* newspaper, she said, printed several letters from others who had also seen the giveaway bottle.

One of the most talked-about anomalies is the American flag that the astronauts hammered into the lunar surface. This was photographed fully extended, and fluttering, despite there being no wind on the Moon. The allegation is that it must have been filmed in a breeze on Earth.

Perhaps the most interesting question is this: if there was nobody *on* the Moon, who filmed Neil Armstrong, supposedly the first man on the Moon, stepping down onto the surface? That seems unanswerable.

But NASA uses a simple argument to rebut all this detail. As early as June 1977, they said that the truth of the Moon landings is shown by rock samples brought back to Earth. The Apollo programme collected pounds of Moon rock and scientists across the globe agree that all this stuff came from the Moon. Most Moon rocks are more than 200 million years older than the oldest Earth rocks, and could not have been formed under conditions here.

Another thing NASA says proves the Moon landings were real is that, from lift-off to splashdown, the programme was scrutinised live by thousands of scientists worldwide, as well as by hostile foreign media who would have trumpeted any lies or failure.

Over the years, the detailed comments about the alleged photographic trickery have also been rejected. The harsh lighting in some pictures does indeed look like a movie effect: and it is true that a single-source light is often used in space films. But the technique is copied from nature (the sun). What's more, sunlight in space is as bright as that on Earth, so the dim light of the stars does not register.

The hotspots on the surface come from anomalies in the photographic lenses that create a luminescence around photographed shadows, and the crosshair effect is caused by overexposed prints bleaching out the 0.1 mm-thick crosshairs.

The backgrounds in photographs were never actually identical. There is no atmosphere on the Moon to make faraway objects look faint, so they appear sharp and clear. Nearby 'hills' are actually distant mountains.

The flag apparently blowing in a stiff breeze had a horizontal rod along its top to hold it in an extended position and prevent it falling straight down in the wind-less vacuum of space. It appeared to be rippled because it had been squashed in storage. In a still picture the ripples do look like a wind effect, except that all the pictures show identical ripples.

To the tricky problem of who it was who photo-graphed *from the Moon* the first man to step onto the Moon, the answer is plain: cameras on the Lunar Module recorded Neil Armstrong descending onto the lunar surface. He switched them on while still on the ladder, so that 600 million people could watch him take 'one small step' and 'one giant leap' down onto the surface.

Researchers have found no newspaper letters about the mystery rolling Coke bottle. To be generous I will suggest that, having stayed up late, the lady in question may have been overtired. Except that, as many Oz viewers recall, the landing took place in the middle of the Australian day.

Water Fluoridation

A Soviet Plot for World Domination?

If there is one person who can be blamed for giving conspiracy theorists a bad name it is General Jack D. Ripper. General Ripper appears in Stanley Kubrick's 1964 satirical film *Dr. Strangelove*, in which he launches a nuclear strike against the Soviet Union because he thinks they are fluoridating American tap water in an 'international communist conspiracy' to 'sap and impurify' his 'precious bodily fluids'.

By 1960, about fifty million Americans were cheerfully drinking fluoridated water. This was a time of extreme Cold War touchiness. In 1962 the Cuban Missile Crisis gave everyone the end-of-the-world willies and it was during this period that *Dr. Strangelove* was in production. What better focus for people's anxieties than the idea that the Soviet government was putting something in the water?

But, as these things do, the accusations about who was actually responsible began to proliferate, and today the claims that fluoride has been added to our tap water to harm not help us are many and various. Like the rumours that the British army put bromide in soldiers' tea during the Second World War to dampen libidos, there's a theory that water fluoridation was devised by a German chemical company to subdue its populace. Other plots are said to involve the sugar or aluminium industries. Some think it is a New World Order conspiracy (*see page 149*) to take over the world and still others that it is an attempt by the government to disguise their failure to provide poor people with proper tooth care.

In fact, the idea that fluoride should be added to drinking water started well over a hundred years ago. It had been established early in the nineteenth century that fluoride is present in teeth and bones, as well as in water, and in 1874 a dietary fluoride supplement was recommended in Germany to prevent tooth rot. In 1892, British doctor and magnificent mutton-chop-wearer Sir James Crichton-Browne told dentists that refined food had reduced the amount of fluoride in the diet, causing teeth to be 'peculiarly liable to decay'.

Then, in 1901, Frederick McKay, a young American dentist from the East Coast, opened a practice in Colorado Springs, Colorado, and was astonished by the chocolate-brown teeth of many of the locals, which contrasted with the urinal-white smiles of the folks back home – a condition that became known as Colorado Brown Stain. Though brown tooth-staining was already a recognised condition, the cause was unknown and McKay was a man on a mission. He researched brown teeth for decades and found this discolouration in other places too. In the South, the distinctive brown smile was known as 'Texas teeth'.

In 1909, a dental researcher, Dr G. V. Black, began collaborating with McKay on the coffee-coloured smile, which he called 'a deformity for life', and fourteen years later, in 1923, McKay confirmed a connection between fluoride and drinking water, when he discovered that the teeth of children in Oakley, Idaho, went brown only after the building of a water pipeline to a nearby spring. In 1931, chemists examining the drinking water found fluoride, finally completing the puzzle. It was high levels of fluoride that was causing people's teeth to go brown. But their discovery also brought some good news, as when the doctor told the man he'd amputated the wrong leg but the other one was getting better. The good news was that these brown teeth proved surprisingly resistant to decay.

It became clear that deliberately introducing fluoride to drinking water at very low levels would significantly reduce dental caries, without causing teeth to go brown. So in 1945 Grand Rapids, Michigan, became the first city in the world to fluoridate its drinking water. After eleven years tooth decay had fallen by more than 60 per cent. McKay and others had changed dentistry from a fill-or-pull business into a prevention-based discipline.

However, since this pioneering work the research has been far from scintillating and doubts have arisen about whether water fluoridation really is a successful preventive measure, a useless and expensive flushing of fivers down the drain, or positively harmful. In 2007 a report by the Nuffield Council on bioethics found that good evidence for or against it was lacking. The US Centers for Disease Control and Prevention, however, called fluoridation one of the ten great public health achievements of the twentieth century, along with vaccination, contraception and understanding the dangers of smoking. In the face of all this contradictory opinion and doubt, conspiracism spread like dental plaque.

Some conspiracy theories are right wing, like the theory that fluoridation is part of a Soviet-inspired plot to implant in America a fiendish health system paid for by taxes, along with further 'harmful' public health programmes such as vaccination and mental health services. Dr Frederick Exner, an anti-fluoridationist from the sixties, put it bluntly: 'Most people are not prepared to believe that fluoridation is a communist plot, and if you say it is, you are successfully ridiculed by the promoters. It is being done, effectively, every day … some of the people on our side are the fluoridators' fifth column.' Even in 1995, conspiracy-theory magazine *Nexus* quoted a person called Charles Elliot Perkins who said: 'Repeated doses of infinitesimal amounts of fluoride will in time reduce an individual's power to resist domination, by slowly poisoning and narcotising a certain area of the brain, and will thus make him submissive to the will of those who wish to govern him.' The jury is still sucking its teeth on this one.

The trouble with all these dire predictions is that since our water has been fluoridated, the Soviet Union has disappeared and nothing terrible seems to have happened to us from drinking tap water. Magazines like *Take a Break* and *OK!* or those homegrown shopping channels do a far better job of reducing people to zombies than a bit of watery Russian fluoride.

'Deadly' Vaccines

In 1998, two days before the end of an uncommonly warm February, a gaggle of journalists arrived for a press conference at one of London's renowned teaching hospitals, the Royal Free, in Hampstead. They were there to hear gastroenterologist and medical researcher Dr Andrew Wakefield discuss a scientific paper, written with twelve colleagues, which was being published the same day in the *Lancet* medical journal.

Dr Wakefield's paper made the radical suggestion that the triple MMR (measles, mumps, rubella) vaccine might be causing serious problems. Eight out of twelve children Wakefield had studied had, he said, developed bowel problems and signs of autism shortly after getting the jab.

In a nod to caution, four eminent Royal Free doctors were at the press conference to point out that, despite the apparent bombshell in Wakefield's paper, more research was needed before any definite conclusions could be reached, and it was 'absolutely essential' that public confidence in the MMR vaccine not be damaged, and that children continue to get the jab, which had been given quite safely to millions around the world for many years, saving countless lives.

But hardly had the journalists opened their notebooks than Wakefield shot dramatically off-piste, urging parents to give their children yearly single inoculations instead of the triple jab, on the ground that the MMR vaccination might be too much for some immune systems.

Newspapers splashed Wakefield's postulations across their front pages under big fat unsubtle headlines, and minus the wise caveats of his more measured medical colleagues. This naturally alarmed parents around the world, some of whom thought they recognised a connection between the jab and their child's autism, the symptoms of which are often noticed at around eighteen months, the same time that the MMR vaccine is generally given. But it is well understood that it's not the vaccination that produces autism in children of about eighteen months old, it's being about eighteen months old. That's the risky thing. Nonetheless, some parents, insisting on a non-existent cause and effect, and perhaps not realising the seriousness of the diseases that the vaccine prevents, decided to give their children no jabs at all, causing a marked drop-off in vaccination rates.

Wakefield's findings could not be, and never were, repeated by other scientists, and a study by the British Medical Association, which examined research from 180 countries, found no evidence that the MMR jab was associated either with autism or inflammatory bowel disease.

The Wakefield church was built on sand, and in due course ten of Dr Wakefield's co-authors disowned the study's conclusions. But the mills of medicine ground slowly and it was not until the end of January 2010, twelve years after his cockamamie report, that Britain's General Medical Council censured Wakefield's serious professional misconduct, calling it 'irresponsible' and 'dishonest'. *The Lancet* announced that it was retracting the 1998 paper and Dr Wakefield was struck off the medical register.

One of the problems with characters like Mr Wakefield is that their intense certitude, along with their white-coat authority, persuades people who are not experts that what they are saying is true. Even if eminent doctors disagree with them, and even if the evidence points in an altogether different direction, some people will still be persuaded. In the age of Facebook and the Twittersphere this can lead to an explosion of knee-jerk conspiracy theories, which may start as niche topics but can quickly 'go viral', with theories that become increasingly elaborate, or split off into mutually contradictory branches.

The original Andrew Wakefield nonsense was quickly inflated in this way. The conspiracy theories into which it developed include the notion that governments are conspiring with the pharmaceutical companies to make dishonest millions under the guise of educating people to the dangers of certain diseases and promoting public health. There is a particularly popular one still doing the rounds, which is the seductive yet baseless allegation that Bill Gates is using vaccination to secretly microchip the whole world (*see page 136*). Why Bill would bother with such a vast and ruinously expensive programme is beyond me; it makes Santa's job look like a picnic. And what is he supposed to be getting out of it?

The problem with some of these medical conspiracy theories is that they cause people to change their behaviour in dangerous ways. Anti-vaxxers (as they have been dubbed) contributed, for instance, to the tripling of European measles outbreaks in 2018, and the worst American outbreak in a generation in 2019.

The anti-vax movement is made up of a lot of different people, from fearful mothers and those attracted to 'natural' remedies, to anti-pharma activists and unbending disbelievers in science and medicine. The movement is growing. In 2020, interactions on posts doubtful of or hostile towards vaccines on six UK Facebook pages went up from 12,000 to 42,000 in one month, though I did read that just twelve people are responsible for nearly all the anti-vax stories online.

Though anti-vaxxers are a small minority they have an especially strident social-media voice. Often it is a highly unpleasant and harmful one. In June 2020, CNN reported that anti-vaxxers had sent vaccine supporters thousands of abusive and violent messages, including racial attacks and death threats. When CNN challenged Facebook over these posts a spokesperson, who for some strange reason asked not to be named, said the company could not take action because vaccine supporters had provided screen shots of the verbal violence, but no links. In 2019, however, weeks after CNN alerted them, Facebook did remove the account of one especially foul-mouthed anti-vaxxer, who had sent suicide instructions to a vaccine supporter.

American cultural critic Mark Molloy says that 'right-wing' posts and QAnon conspiracy theories (*see page*

199) spread easily on Facebook despite supposed bans, showing that Facebook is 'highly partisan'. In a 2020 Axios interview, Facebook chief Mark Zuckerberg responded: 'It's true that partisan content often has kind of a higher percent of people ... engaging with it, commenting on it, liking it.' One might ask why it was not until President Donald Trump's last fortnight in office that Facebook, and also Twitter, saw fit to kick him and his unhinged messages off their platforms.

Facebook is home to two unattractive organisations, Stop Mandatory Vaccination and Children's Health Defense. Children's Health Defense was founded by its chairman, Robert F. Kennedy Jr. It campaigns not just against vaccination, but also wireless communications and fluoridation of tap water (*see page 121*). In 2020, Stop Mandatory Vaccination's Facebook group was at the hub of a controversy concerning the mother of a young boy, who decided against giving him the ortho-dox flu treatment her doctor had prescribed in favour of the anti-vaxxers' recommended but futile treatment of breastmilk, thyme and elderberry. He died. In early 2021, Robert F. Kennedy Jr was finally booted off Instagram.

These groups may smile away such tragedies but this is real human suffering at their door.

During the COVID-19 pandemic, UK acceptance turned out to be much higher than had been feared. Israel led the world in quickly vaccinating its population, and in other countries confidence grew as more people were given the jab. In the UK, which had a very successful vaccine rollout, almost everybody offered the vaccine accepted it with extended, if not open, arms.

The anti-vax movement falsely claims, among other fairy tales, that face masks 'activate' the COVID-19 coronavirus, whatever that is supposed to mean, and a 2020 poll showed that only half of Americans said they would have a COVID-19 jab. But, there again, polls are notoriously unreliable. One said the number of Americans unwilling to be vaccinated was 22 per cent, while another claimed it was 14 per cent. There is a big difference between 50, 22 and 14 per cent. It is important to be as sceptical of apparently authoritative survey statistics as of claims about supposedly harmful vaccines.

Of course, there is no point just shouting at anti-vax parents. If yelling at parents worked, teenagers would be the world's best communicators. What is required is cool-headed exploration of the evidence and its quality. While nobody has died thinking the Moon landings were faked, believing twaddle about vaccines can be extremely dangerous, and has led to tragic preventable death.

Hollow Earth

The Hole Truth

Since Jules Verne's 1864 science-fiction novel *Journey to the Centre of the Earth*, the notion that you might travel to the inside of our planet has fascinated human beings. Unlike the idea that the Earth is flat, the idea that it is hollow doesn't seem obvious. Nevertheless, there is a conspiracy theory based on this interesting fancy.

The story goes that the hollow centre of the Earth is inhabited by a race of superior beings, where they, along with some Vikings and Nazis, live in a kind of paradise. These advanced tribes consider themselves 'guardians of the planet' and send flying saucers out to monitor us surface-dwellers to prevent nuclear war.

The hollow Earth theory has its origins in the beliefs of the Ancient Greeks, Tibetan Buddhists and Christians, but it was during the Age of Reason that the theory was first proposed as something more than a metaphor. Edmond Halley, the comet man (1656–1742), came to the conclusion that funny compass readings were caused by the Earth being a hollow shell inhabited by all kinds of creatures. This idea took off and Swiss mathematician Leonhard Euler (pronounced *oiler*: 1707–1783) decided that this hollow Earth must have a 600-mile-wide sun at its centre. Being blind, he never saw this sun, and came to his conclusions using what he said was physics. He explained that the internal sun supported the advanced civilisations who lived down there, with their own cultures and convenience stores, and concluded that there were entrances to the core at both the North and South Poles, making the Earth a bit like a cored apple. Edgar Allan Poe, Baudelaire, Jules Verne and Edgar Rice Burroughs all saw great potential in the hollow-Earth concept.

US army officer John Cleves Symmes, Jr (1780–1829) took up the idea and tried to get Congress to fund an expedition to find the bottom hole – by which I mean the one at the South Pole – but without luck. When he died, his disciple Jeremiah Reynolds carried on the work, and in 1829 drummed up enough money for the voyage.

Hitler is also rumoured to have been a fan of the hole-in-the-Pole theory, and sent expeditions to Antarctica to look into it – not look into the *hole*, to *investigate*, I mean.

In 1947 polar explorer Admiral Richard Byrd reported in his private journal that he had actually gone down the hole and entered 'the centre of the great unknown'. He found thriving advanced civilisations on this trip but was attacked by Nazi flying saucers that burst out of the ocean and wiped out half his fleet. He was later questioned about details by Washington officials, who kept a big desk between themselves and him just in case. He claimed they told him to stop discussing the hollow Earth at once.

But, in fact, Byrd was a late arrival in the centre of the Earth. Norwegian sailor Olaf Jansen had already told people he had sailed through the North Pole entrance in 1830, describing the place he found as 'Eden'. It was in a beautiful valley, 'yet, in fact, it is on the loftiest mountain plateau of the Inner Continent'. Work *that* one out.

This idea of a secret garden is threaded through literature and religion, from the earliest ages. It seems to exert a mysterious hold over the human imagination, like Cockaigne, the land of plenty in medieval myths, or the Big Rock Candy Mountain in that song, where there 'ain't no snow', and the trees produce cigarettes, and the cops all have wooden legs. Nowadays, with global heating and modern medicine, there really ain't no snow, and cigarettes kill you, and the cops have great big guns. But Olaf truly spoilt the bucolic appeal by going on about the twelve-foot-tall 'super humans' who he said lived in the garden. According to others, these characters walked the 'Inner Earth' upside-down, with their feet glued to the ceiling, and had 'grapes as big as peaches and apples as big as your head' – not what you imagine the Garden of Eden to be like, really.

American Rodney Cluff, author of the self-published *World Top Secret: Our Earth IS Hollow!* (2014), explains that whenever there is a large earthquake the Earth 'rings like a bell, and you can find this in all the scientific literature ...' His thinking is that since a bell is hollow, so is the Earth. You can't fault that, really. He says the skin of the Earth is just 800 miles thick, and agrees that in the centre is a small sun that supplies 'light and life' to the interior world, which contains, among others, the lost tribes of Israel, some Vikings and Hitler. Naturally enough, the inhabitants have flying-saucer technology.

Rodney elaborates on the entrances to the inner world: 'Near the poles are openings that go into the interior. We call them "polar openings",' he says helpfully. Asked by SunOnline for his views on the contradictory flat-Earth theory, he said he didn't know how the flat-Earthers could be so confused. They were obviously wrong – the world was not flat but hollow. 'They reject all the evidence,' he said.

I rather took to Rodney. He wears striped T-shirts and is quietly spoken and polite. He has planned a number of trips on an icebreaker to locate the hollow Earth's opening at the North Pole, but, as so often happens with these things, he has been plagued by bad luck and has not yet made it. Presumably he remains hopeful.

In 2016, there was a 'polar-opening' breakthrough, when hollow-Earth supporters showed that a huge hole at the North Pole, leading straight to the centre of the Earth, had been covered up by the US government and NASA. YouTube conspiracy theorists secureteam10 said that, 'Every single satellite image we have of the North Pole shows a massive hole or a blackout hole put there to hide whatever's underneath.'

The entrances to the hollow Earth are also said to be visible on Google Earth, but when I had a look, squinting as hard as I could, I found little except fuzzy smudges. Apparently, pictures of the secret entrances are deliberately blurred by the superpowers, who conspire with reptilians (*see page 192*), Atlanteans and aliens to stop gossip about the holes getting out, which is understandable.

A couple of physical challenges face the hollow-Earth conspiracy theorists, however. First of all, if the Earth is hollow, its density and therefore its gravity must be much less than they appear to be. But, if this were true, we'd all have to tie ourselves down with lead weights, along with our fridges, cars and pets, or we'd all float off into space. Neither is it made clear what is holding up the incredibly thin shell of the outer Earth. The Earth is not a perfect sphere; it is an oblate spheroid, slightly fatter at the equator, where it is 12,756 km (7,926 miles) in diameter, like a huge tangerine, or a jam doughnut someone has sat on. At 800 miles, the shell of the hollow Earth is only about a tenth this width. If this were really the case, though, you'd need huge bicycle-spoke things inside to stop it collapsing in on itself like a huge chocolate balloon. Maybe I'll send Rodney Cluff a letter to ask him what he thinks about this. There again, I notice it's time for my medicine. Where did I put the corkscrew?

COVID-19 Conspiracy Theories Go Viral

On 31 December 2019, the World Health Organization received reports of a cluster of unusual cases of viral pneumonia in the Chinese city of Wuhan. The newly discovered virus was surmised to be closely related to bat and pangolin coronaviruses. The term 'coronavirus' refers to the fringe of spiky blobs on the virus's surface, which look vaguely like the solar corona – the halo around the sun. It was this novel virus, given the name SARS-CoV-2, that was causing the highly infectious and extremely nasty new disease: COVID-19. Cases quickly spread outside China and in March 2020 the World Health Organization declared the disease a pandemic.

According to Professor Eric Oliver from the University of Chicago, the most popular conspiracy theories are medical, and, predictably, several COVID-19 conspiracy theories soon began spreading across social media. An invisible lethal illness like COVID-19 makes people highly apprehensive, uncertain and anxious, says Professor Oliver, which causes some people – those who demand simple answers to complex political and health questions – to find in conspiracy theories the reassuringly uncomplicated explanations they seek.

Among the top COVID-19 conspiracy theories are: 1) that the virus doesn't actually exist; 2) that Bill Gates is the cause; 3) that 5G is the cause; and 4) that it is a planned occurrence plotted by the 'deep state' or Big Pharma. Only one of these could be true, so the question is: what is the evidence for each of them?

The concept of the 'non-existent virus' can be found all over the internet, and in the real world. In the summer of 2020, more than 10,000 protesters who believed coronavirus is a hoax squashed up together, maskless, at a so-called 'Unite for Freedom' rally in London, while Skin Kerr salon in Bootle put up posters and online posts telling customers that staff were not wearing masks because 'You can't catch what doesn't exist'. The idea of the disease being an invention was also pursued in an Italian video, watched on Facebook something like a million times. Voicing the video was an Italian anti-vaccine activist named Stefano Montanari, who claimed the pandemic would 'continue to be totally made up' until a vaccine was developed that would 'bring money and corruption into the already full pockets of some'. The trouble is, there is no evidence that the pandemic was totally 'made up', and an enormous amount of evidence that it was not. There are records in every country of the numbers of people who have contracted the disease, and we all know of people who have caught COVID-19, including Prime Minister Boris Johnson and former American President Donald Trump, so the idea that it isn't there is immediately disprovable. In any case, the theory is half baked: surely anyone working a conspiracy of this sort would have the money-making vaccine ready *before* 'making up' the pandemic.

The tendency of some people to disbelieve or minimise warnings of real threats, such as a pandemic, may be partly explained by something called 'normalcy bias' or 'normality bias'. Also known by the less fancy names 'analysis paralysis' and 'the ostrich effect', this cognitive bias prevents people from accepting what is coming. This, in turn, causes them to fail to plan or act to protect themselves.

What about conspiracy theory number two: the Bill Gates theory? This claims that the coronavirus pandemic is merely a plausible cover for a purported Gates scheme: to develop a vaccine containing a microchip, which he plans to inject into everyone in the world so we can all be tracked, thus creating what has been called 'a vaccine-enabled surveillance state'.

This idea seems to have come from the Bill and Melinda Gates Foundation having funded a university study into a possible vaccine-delivery device. This accurate information appears then to have been fused with another piece of accurate information: Gates's involvement in research into cloud-based storage of medical or personal documents, a so-called 'digital identity', which would be accessible only with the consent of the owner. The muddled conflation of these two facts has resulted in the fiction that a digital tracker would somehow be injected into everybody. In fact, nothing would be injected into anybody, never mind something that could be used to track a person's location. Such nanotechnology doesn't exist, though there has been much chatter about so-called 'quantum dots' – molecule-size particles engineered so that a smartphone might identify them. But this concept is in the foothills of research and could not be used for anything like tracking people from inside an injected vaccine. In any case, if being tracked is what's bothering you, get rid of your smartphone.

Gates was linked to another coronavirus vaccine claim in a popular YouTube video that mentions the Pirbright Institute, which gets some of its funding from the Gates Foundation. Pirbright is a research establishment in Surrey that holds a patent for just such a vaccine. But for some reason, the video forgets to mention that this institute studies infectious diseases in farm animals, and that the vaccine patent is actually for a coronavirus affecting poultry. People have either jumped to ludicrous conclusions, or been purposely misleading.

Deliberate mendacity seems to have been behind the head of the Russian Communist Party referring to an American plan for 'a covert mass chip implantation which they may in time resort to under the pretext of a mandatory vaccination against coronavirus'. But it's not only Russia that has produced such fairy tales. In the US, Roger Stone – described variously as a conservative political consultant, a lobbyist and a 'mendacious windbag' – favoured a different conspiracy theory: that Bill Gates and others were using the virus for microchipping people to find out whether they had been tested for COVID-19. No evidence was cited by the communist gentleman, nor by the capitalist one, because there is none. In any case,

Stone suffered an unfortunate blow to his reliability when he was convicted of witness tampering and lying to investigators, before being sentenced to more than three years in prison, a punishment later commuted by his old friend Donald Trump.

Despite the logical contradictions and obvious COVID-19 falsehoods, a YouGov poll indicated that 28 per cent of Americans were persuaded that Bill Gates 'wants to use vaccines to implant microchips in people'. Among Republicans, it was 44 per cent. This seems a vast number of people to be basing their ideas of reality upon nothing but rumour.

Now we come to the role of 5G in the COVID-19 pandemic. 5G is the fifth-generation mobile-phone technology that companies started to introduce globally in 2019. For quite some time conspiracy theories about the harmfulness to health of 5G had been floating about online, and COVID-19 gave them a new illness to attach themselves to.

One claim was that 5G makes people more vulnerable to catching COVID-19 by suppressing their immune system. It was said to do this by heating them up. Dr Simon Clarke, associate professor in cellular microbiology at the University of Reading, explained the impossibility of this idea using simple words. The theory was, he explained, 'complete rubbish ... 5G is nowhere near strong enough to heat people up', possibly raising his eyes to heaven as he said so.

The obviousness of this seemed not to have seeped into the psyches of some of the more aggressive anti-5G crowd. In April 2020 an Openreach engineer named Dylan Farrell was driving home after a busy shift. As he pulled up in his van at a roundabout in Thurmaston, near Leicester, a man began screaming at him through his side window. 'You've got no morals,' he yelled. '5G is killing us all!' Frightened that this person was intent on assaulting him, Farrell locked the door before quickly driving away.

Other 5G engineers across the country also revealed that they had been shouted at. The *Guardian* reported one engineer being abused on three separate occasions in one week, finally finding himself on the end of 'a physically threatening verbal tirade from a man who coated his face in spittle'. This poor engineer then went down with COVID-19 symptoms.

At about the same time as these attacks on these men doing innocuous jobs, videos began appearing on social media showing seventy or more mobile-phone masts being vandalised across the country, most of which had nothing to do with 5G and were serving the UK's Emergency Services Network, a 4G system that keeps police, ambulance and fire-brigade communications going.

Of the top COVID-19 conspiracy theories, the last is that the disease outbreak was not a natural pandemic but a 'plandemic', the result of deliberate viral 'manipulation' in a laboratory. Unfortunately, much of the diagnostic advice in one very widely shared video is simply wrong, as is a good deal of what purports to be 'medical information' about the virus and the way it is spread.

Nonetheless, the hashtag #Plandemic has been used many thousands of times, and the video watched millions of times. YouTube and other social media platforms finally took down several versions.

But does this sort of inaccuracy really matter that much? The answer is yes, as it may harm not only those who believe it, but others too. We are all mistaken in our beliefs some of the time but usually these mistakes are trivial. Nobody has perished from sitting at home believing the Earth to be flat or that kissing frogs will produce a handsome prince. It doesn't matter what you *think*, it's what you *do* that counts, and false conspiracy theories about a potentially deadly virus are likely to make some people do dangerous things.

Many people who fail to cross-check claims they see presented by persuasive speakers online and in the media take some of these demonstrably false claims very seriously.

Florida taxi driver Brian Lee Hitchens was in his forties when, in May 2020, he and his wife fell ill with the symptoms of COVID-19. Brian told the media from his hospital bed that they did not seek help until it was too late because, 'We thought the government was using it to distract us, or it was to do with 5G, so we didn't follow the rules or seek help sooner.' He came to regret his actions after his wife, who was being ventilated in the ward next door, died.

Anti-vaccination proponents are a very small minority of the American population but their social-media voice is loud and their influence wide. After all, the internet is a global phenomenon and when America sneezes, the world catches cold. For example, in 2020, a YouGov poll found that 16 per cent of Britons said they would refuse vaccination, though in the end nearly everyone in the UK gladly accepted the jab.

As well as denial of its dangers, and twaddle about its causes, various useless treatments for COVID-19 have also been circulating on social media, and were noticeable in the White House press briefings and on the Twitter feed of former President Trump. Trump favoured a couple of ideas. One was a malaria medication called hydroxychloroquine. 'What do you have to lose?' he said on 3 April 2020, a few weeks before Brian Hitchens and his wife fell ill.

In October 2020, speaking about COVID-19, Trump mentioned the effect of masks: 'Just the other day they [the Centers for Disease Control and Prevention] came out with a statement that 85 per cent of the people that wear masks catch it.' The CDC had said no such thing, because it was complete rubbish. The president seemed to be making it up as he went along.

Later in April, he decided to talk about ultraviolet light, which he had heard could kill the virus by being somehow put *inside* the body. He was also intrigued by household cleaners: 'And then I see the disinfectant where it knocks it out in a minute. One minute. And is there a way we can do something like that, by injection inside or almost a cleaning?' said the President of the United States of America.

Doctors at New York's Elmhurst Hospital told the

BBC they found themselves having to treat acutely ill patients who had swallowed disinfectant. One of the medics, Dr Duncan Maru, explained that staff were spending time trying to debunk misinformation when they could be treating patients.

Having said in 2009 that he thought vaccines could be 'very dangerous', Trump quietly got the COVID jab in January 2021. He later described it as 'unpainful' (painless?) and, in a remarkable change of tune, told his followers, '… Everybody go and get your shot.'

To tackle the spread of these nonsensical and potentially harmful COVID-19 conspiracy theories, social media companies drew up new rules. Facebook said they had taken down 'hundreds of thousands' of posts, including contradictory claims that COVID-19 is non-existent, and that it was caused by 5G, as well as numerous fake 'cures'. YouTube says it does not allow promotion of dangerous 'cures' and has policies against COVID-19 misinformation.

But what is the best way to unpick fact and fiction in COVID-19 conspiracy theories, or to have a rational discussion with someone who is convinced that COVID-19 does not exist or that Bill Gates or 5G is behind it? It can be a tough job, as these theories sometimes spring not only from a misunderstanding of the rules of inference, but from deep feelings of powerlessness, anxiety, resentment and indignation. Many conspiracy theories are at root reassuring cowboys-and-Indians stories about supposed goodies and baddies, and about as accurate a portrayal of the truth. What is more, rational argument can find itself up against a barrage of emotion. All the same, there are some points that may help you to have a civilised discussion about all these ideas with a person who does not share your views.

Like many conspiracy theories, COVID-19 conspiracy theories are often a mixture of truth and falsity. It is easy for a conspiracy theory superspreader to make arguments persuasive by starting with scientific facts and only slowly wandering up the yellow brick road of fantasy. Explaining to them that you agree with certain facts but that these don't lead to the conclusions they are proposing can occasionally help someone to see there is something wrong with their argument. There is no way, for example, that 5G can be the cause of a virus that doesn't exist. That is like a defendant claiming he didn't assault his neighbour because he wasn't anywhere near him, and anyway it was self-defence. It is very tempting to feel superior to obvious mistakes of this kind but you should avoid being smug, because it is not unheard of to discover that there is something wrong with *your own* argument.

Of course, not everybody is amenable to rational discussion, and explanations about the lack of evidence for someone's belief might fall upon stony ground. Supporters of health conspiracy theories may see lack of evidence simply as proof that the conspirators are especially good at what they do. The less evidence there is, they might say, the truer the conspiracy theory must be. This fault of logic leads to absurdity. You could point out that lack of evidence for the tooth fairy is not proof that the tooth fairy exists. Simple though this proposition sounds, however, some people find it hard to grasp.

All you can do is remain polite and friendly, challenge the evidence you are presented with and check the reliability of any sources you are quoted. A wild claim on Facebook or Twitter with no link to an authoritative source is not evidence, and it is surely unwise to base your life-and-death decisions upon such flimsy conjecture.

Finally, you might ask, 'What evidence would you need to change your mind?' This excellent question will reveal how deeply your interlocutor has considered the pros and cons of their argument. It is such a good question you should ask it of yourself. Often.

VII

BIG BROTHER IS WATCHING YOU

Inside Jobs and Government Dirty Tricks

Things are not always what they seem;
first appearances deceive many.

—PHÆDRUS

New World Order

Behind many of the most intense political and financial upheavals the world has seen over the centuries lurks a secret conspiracy orchestrated by a cabal of sinister front organisations. These include the world's major religions, including Christians, Jews and Muslims, the Illuminati (*see page 187*), international banking cliques, the Freemasons (*see page 182*) and, naturally enough, aliens (*see pages 29, 33 and 37*). Backed by these powerful players, a gradualist plan for world domination is gaining such speed and strength that sovereign nation-states are soon to be swept away and replaced by a totalitarian, globalist, one world government. At least, that's the idea.

This all started during the latter part of the nineteenth century, when English-born South African mining mogul, politician and white supremacist Cecil Rhodes began pushing for the reordering of the world, in a scheme he called 'England everywhere'. In 1877, at the age of just twenty-three, Rhodes announced his desire to fund a secret cabal of the chosen few, to be known as the Society of the Elect, which would gradually 'absorb the wealth of the world' and work for 'the extension of British rule throughout the world … the ultimate recovery of the

United States of America as an integral part of the British Empire ... and, finally, the foundation of so great a Power as to render wars impossible, and promote the best interests of humanity'.

Despite its sugar coating, Rhodes's undemocratic imperialist plan got only as far as the Rhodes Scholarship, founded to foster peace among the great powers by allowing an entrusted few from outside England to study free at Oxford University. Rhodes scholars have included American singer-songwriter Kris Kristofferson, who wrote the hit 'Help Me Make It Through the Night', and a chap named Bill Clinton, who became president and found himself in hot water over some marks on an intern's dress. Whether this pair were up to snuff for world takeovers is an interesting question.

Since the time of Cecil Rhodes, the definition of 'New World Order' has changed. It has been used to cheer populations during periods of disruption in the global balance of power, when rich countries have worked together for the transnational management of multinational problems that are too complex for single nation-states to tackle alone. After the First World War, for example, when the embryonic League of Nations seemed to herald a lasting international peace, the phrase was used hopefully – though the wiser and more sceptical were not overly confident. The term was used again in a positive sense after the massive political and financial reorganisation that followed the Second World War; the triumph, you might think, of hope over experience.

In the more prosperous 1960s, another time of political

upheaval, the phrase underwent an about-turn, as members of the John Birch Society – described either as 'rabidly far-right extremists' or 'patriotic friends of democracy', depending on your viewpoint – suggested that some gentlemen's clubs and 'think tanks' were Illuminati fronts (*see page 187*) plotting one world government as part of their plan for a New World Order. Others warned of an age-old scheme funded, they said, by an international banking cabal, and run by the 'Anglo-American Establishment', which would impose an evil oligarchy of wealth distributors, immigration lovers and international-trade-deal merchants, to force upon the people a one-world-government mix of 'super-capitalism' and communism.

The phrase 'New World Order' was given a cheerful spin once more after the Cold War, when Mikhail Gorbachev and George H. W. Bush promised a new age of bi-national cooperation; but this failed to come off and the term seemed doomed.

After a period on life support, however, the cliché has recently received the kiss of life, though reverting once again to its gloomy character. It continues to crop up in right-wing conspiracy theories, the brainchildren of anti-government tub-thumpers and fundamentalist apocalyptic millennial Christians, who denounce globalisation, international cooperation, the European monetary union, transnational trade deals and the International Monetary Fund. They predict a forthcoming New World Order as prophesied in the Book of Revelation. At the 'end time', say the Bible wavers, great tribulation will herald the second coming of Christ, along with a visit from the Antichrist, in the person of either the United Nations' secretary-general or the president of the European Union. This struggle will be followed by a golden age of peace and harmony, lovely low petrol prices and the welcome return of segregated golf clubs.

Finally, of course, comes the inevitable all-encompassing New World Order conspiracy theory. This says that the world will be run by visiting aliens and Reptilians from inside the hollow Earth (*see page 131*). Having taken on human form and insinuated themselves into positions of power in government, religion, industry and commerce, the extraterrestrials are already – it would appear – conspiring with a secret US government agency codenamed 'Majestic 12' to develop military-grade flying saucers at Area 51 (*see page 37*). The aliens' scheme to impose its New World Order is now nearing completion, and a cover-up policed by Men in Black (*see page 33*) is concealing all this from the people.

One difficulty for researchers looking for the truth in the briar patch of New World Order conspiracy theories, many of them generations old, is that its aims cannot be both communist *and* capitalist, Christian *and* Reptilian, Anglo-American *and* extraterrestrial: the different explanations are mutually contradictory. The answer to these logical impossibilities, cheerfully adopted by some, is to apply 'doublethink', which George Orwell describes in his novel *Nineteen Eighty-Four* as the ability to hold two contradictory beliefs in your mind at the same time, and accept both of them.

9/11

Attack on the World Trade Center

At about 1.45 on the afternoon of Tuesday, 11 September 2001, a jumbo jet flew into the top of one of the World Trade Center towers in New York, causing a large fire. Minutes later a similar plane crashed into the other tower. In less than two hours both buildings had collapsed into their own footprint. Concrete, computers, people and everything else were visibly pulverised in mid-air, and the towers' steel frames dismembered. The debris poured down as a dense dust that spread across town like a pyroclastic flow, engulfing everything in its way.

These hijacked passenger planes were two of four that were flown into or towards buildings that day. Of the two others, one hit the Pentagon, in Virginia, and the other crashed in a field in Pennsylvania, on its way to Washington, DC. This was only because passengers overcame the hijackers, who were, the government said, part of a conspiracy of nineteen al-Qaeda terrorists. What became known as 9/11 was the deadliest terrorist attack in history, and Britain lost more of its people than any other country but the USA.

The company that handled security for the World Trade Center had had the complex on high alert for some time, under its director Marvin Bush, brother of the then president. But New York newspaper *Newsday* reported that Dara Coard, who was in charge of security at Tower One (the North Tower), said bomb-sniffing dogs at the building had been abruptly removed from the complex on the Thursday before the attack.

The weekend before the disaster, WTC employee Scott Forbes, who worked on the ninety-seventh floor of the South Tower (Tower Two), described a total abandonment of security, owing to a complete power-cut for some thirty hours on 8 and 9 September. Nothing like this had ever happened before, and it meant that all security cameras were off and all electronic security passes were ineffective. For the first time ever, anybody could come or go into the building without check. And they did. Forbes reported seeing strange people who looked like 'engineers' in overalls coming and going for days with huge toolboxes and large spools of wire.

Another employee, Gary Corbett, said that people claiming to be part of 'guided tours' were making their way into 'secured areas' during the power-down, which he remembered starting on the Friday night and lasting until about four o'clock on Sunday afternoon.

On Tuesday, 11 September, having worked the weekend, Scott Forbes was at his nearby home when the attacks happened. Watching from a distance, he immediately wondered whether any of what he had seen at the weekend was connected with the disaster unfolding in front of him.

Explosive collapse and fire caused destruction of all the buildings in the World Trade Center complex; the clean-up would last nearly a year. Quite illegally, the authorities removed the debris from the site before it could be examined as, or for, evidence. Michael Bloomberg, deep-pocketed businessman and longtime mayor of New York City, defended this action by saying: 'Just looking at a piece of metal generally doesn't tell you anything.' The 185,000 tons of steel remnants were sold to China and India.

Before 9/11, fire had never caused the total collapse of a steel-framed high-rise, but now it had happened three times. The Twin Towers and another skyscraper, known as Building 7, had all collapsed straight down in an unresisted 'free fall' acceleration.

All this was undeniably peculiar, and conspiracy theorists soon popped up with various ideas. The most persistent objections to the official account came not from a bunch of wild-eyed oddballs, but from a group of architects and engineers, who said that physics simply would not allow what was said to have happened.

The group's founder, architect Richard Gage, an expert in fireproof steel-frame buildings, said the 'sudden and spontaneous' collapse of the towers would have been impossible without a precisely timed, controlled demolition that took out the major supporting columns.

For seven minutes before its collapse, orange molten metal could be seen pouring out of WTC 2, and metal remained molten throughout the debris area, indicating temperatures far higher than would be expected in a disaster of this kind. It looked as if this metal was the by-product of a thermite reaction used to weaken the structure. Thermite and nano-thermite are very fast and unusually hot explosive materials used by the military. Unreacted nano-thermitic material has been discovered in many WTC dust samples.

Just before collapse, numerous high-velocity jets of dark debris – clearly visible in photographs and video – were being ejected horizontally up to 150 metres (500 feet), or fifteen bus lengths, from several floors of the building, many floors *below* the areas of damage. These are signs of explosive destruction of vital members.

Live television news cameras were visibly shaken by bomb-like seismic activity, which was recorded by instruments *after* the planes hit but *before* the buildings collapsed. At the start of the collapse of the South Tower a Fox News reporter said: 'There is an explosion at the base of the building … white smoke from the bottom … something happened at the base of the building. Then another explosion.' Many people, including firefighters, heard and saw huge explosions on the lower floors of the first tower, including the lobby. Two dust-covered and bloody firefighters who had been inside the building told a reporter they heard at least three loud explosions before the entire lobby collapsed in on them. One put it like this: 'You're in the building trying to help people and it's exploding on you inside the building.' Firefighter Edward Cachia said: '[We] thought there was like an internal detonation – explosives – because it went in succession, boom, boom, boom, boom, and then the tower came down.'

Though it had some small scattered fires, Building 7, a forty-seven-storey skyscraper near the Twin Towers, was fairly undamaged after their collapse but itself collapsed about seven hours later, imploding in the same way, rapidly falling through what ought to have been the path of greatest resistance. A symmetrical collapse of this kind is a physical impossibility unless most or all of the building's support columns have first been destroyed. Before it fell, witnesses saw people backing away saying, 'They're going to "pull" the building.' Then they heard a countdown.

Billionaire Larry Silverstein, CEO of Silverstein Properties, who acquired the complex just a few weeks before the 9/11 attacks, was not in the building when the Twin Towers collapsed. He later told an interviewer that he got a call from the Fire Department commander telling him the fire in Building 7 could not be contained, and 'they made the decision to pull it'. If you are going to demolish a huge skyscraper like Building 7, how long would it take to track down the experts and get the cables and explosives in the right place?

The architects and engineers group said that overwhelming evidence pointed to the Twin Towers and Building 7 having been destroyed in just such a controlled explosive demolition. But something like this takes planning and much preparation. If the destruction of the World Trade Center was the result of a controlled demolition, then some of what happened on 11 September 2001 would have been planned by 'some sort of an inside group', it is claimed.

Interestingly, many influential people had been warned not to fly by plane that day. Some who worked in the

World Trade Center decided to go to the dentist, or had meetings moved across town, or to other states. San Francisco Mayor Willie Brown said his 'airport security' gave him a warning late on Monday evening, just hours before the attack.

Steve Bannon, the former chief strategist for President Donald Trump, has said: 'The real opposition is the media, and the way to deal with them is to flood the zone with shit.' To distract attention from the more persuasive theories, a leaf was taken from his book of tactics and a whole lot of other conspiracy theories got out there, some crazier-sounding than others.

Some said the planes that hit the Towers were digital replicas, and that phone calls from passengers reporting their hijack before they crashed into the Pentagon had been made by 'voice morphing'. The gorgeously named Major General Albert Stubblebine, commanding general of the US Army Intelligence and Security Command, claimed, apparently correctly, that all security cameras at the Pentagon had been turned off that day; he also said a 'missile', not a plane, had struck the Pentagon. To the regret of some truth seekers, Stubblebine was revealed also to be keen on training an elite corps of 'super soldiers' with 'the ability to become invisible at will and walk through walls'. This is the sort of friendly witness a barrister hesitates to call.

All the same, on 16 May 2006, the government were obliged to release a video from outside the Pentagon. The image of something striking the building is very brief, it is taken from a bad angle and is of poor quality. The thing said to be a plane is little more than a blurred white streak and, whatever it is, seems to come in on a horizontal trajectory, close to the ground. It raises as many questions as it answers.

To understand 9/11, say investigators, you must go back to 1997, when a think tank called the Project for the New American Century (PNAC) was formed. Founders included Dick Cheney, Donald Rumsfeld, John Bolton and Paul Wolfowitz, all of whom would, oddly enough, later become famous names in US neoconservative politics. PNAC promoted 'American global leadership', military strength and 'moral clarity'. Its members believed a 'radical overhaul' of US military forces was required around the globe, but realised that their ideas would have to be implemented salami style – a slice at a time – to avoid political discomfort and social resistance. Things could, however, be done much faster if there were to be what they called, in a now-infamous document, a 'catastrophic and catalysing event like a new Pearl Harbor'.

After the dust had settled Hugo Chavez, president of Venezuela at the time, remarked that there was a strengthening hypothesis that it was the 'US imperial power' that had planned and carried out this tragic terrorist attack against its own people and the citizens of the world. He wondered why, but only rhetorically. His answer was that it had been to justify the aggressions immediately unleashed on Afghanistan and Iraq.

Is this what happened?

The Great Brexit-rigging Conspiracy

In 2016, shortly before the European withdrawal (Brexit) referendum, a YouGov poll of the British public showed there was enormous mistrust of British officialdom, including the media and government. Vast numbers said they thought Brexit had been fixed, that MI5 had infiltrated key organisations, and that the BBC and the main commercial television channels were conspiring to frame the debate in favour of a 'remain' vote.

Populations worldwide have long been divided into those who repeatedly vote for authoritarian rule and those who prefer liberal freedoms. Approaching Brexit, many in Britain felt they were no longer represented by their politicians, but were being 'managed'. While plenty of British people thought there was much good to be said for Europe, others believed the secret decision-making about their lives by distant faceless appointees, whom they could not vote out, was undemocratic. When the Greek finance minister suggested that the European Council's secret meetings should be streamed live, Euro-officials went a funny colour.

As to the Brexit referendum, something like half of those who described themselves as Brexiteers said they thought it was 'probably true' that the referendum outcome had been pre-determined by a conspiratorial 'pro-Europe Establishment'. In contrast, only 11 per cent of Remainers thought the vote would be rigged. Leavers pointed to a multi-million-pound 'factsheet' sent out to all voters by government, which they claimed was biased. The social media #usepens hashtag even urged them to sign their ballot papers not with the official polling-station pencil but with a pen, to prevent their vote being rubbed out by an army of Remainers with strong elbows. Quite what the Brexiteers believed afterwards, when the opposite result was announced, one can only guess. I suppose it depends what evidence they had for their original opinion, and what each person thought 'rigged' meant.

That's the trouble with opinion polls: you get very different results depending on how you phrase and order questions. If you ask, 'Do you think some Europe ministers may have lied in the past?' honest respondents are going to have to answer yes. We have all probably lied in the past, especially when we were children.

On the question of MI5 working with the UK government to try to stop Britain leaving the EU, the answer was predictable. MI5 always attracts suspicion, because the organisation is very touchy about admitting or denying anything. Twenty-eight per cent of Brexiteers suspected the intelligence community had been pushing a Remain agenda in the run-up to Brexit. Only 16 per cent of Remainers thought so, though that seems quite a lot. Quite what their evidence was for this idea I do not know.

More than a third of Brexiteers believed broadcasters were trying to interfere with the vote, three times as many as the tenth of Remainers who thought this. These views reflected the general rightward tilt of those who believe the government, aliens, Men in Black and so on are out to get them. The Left, though, has not been free of its own conspiracy theories. While it is conceivable that there was a conspiracy to tip the Brexit referendum into a leave vote, some have suggested that the unpublicised working together of various shadowy Brexit-supporting groups is just as likely to have had a sinister effect on the result. For example, Brexit campaign group Leave.EU controversially worked alongside Cambridge Analytica, a now-dead political consultancy, which had worked on Donald Trump's 2016 election campaign, and was at the centre of the storm over use of Facebook data.

Interviewed by a House of Commons committee, whistle-blower Christopher Wylie, who helped set up Cambridge Analytica, as well as Canadian-based technology company AggregateIQ, alleged that AIQ was essentially an arm of Cambridge Analytica, and was kept separate partly to hide any links between the two. The money man behind both AggregateIQ and Cambridge Analytica was US billionaire Robert Mercer, who was also Donald Trump's biggest election campaign donor. Wylie claimed that AIQ was part of a scheme to help Vote Leave get around the law on political spending limits during the Brexit campaign. AIQ denied any wrongdoing, saying that it worked 'in full compliance within all legal and regulatory requirements in all jurisdictions where it operates'.

This wasn't the only case of foreign interest in Brexit, and when the University of Edinburgh found that more than four hundred Twitter accounts had been used before the referendum as 'Russian propaganda tools', the true size of the problem began to become clear. The claim was that Russia would be only too delighted to see the EU weakened by the loss of member states such as the UK. Facebook said that any Russian propaganda was not significant.

Photographs of President Trump grinning broadly beside various British Brexiteers further highlighted the global links between populist politicians, businessmen and other Eurosceptic movers and shakers.

In 2021 German historian Helene von Bismarck described British populism as 'a political method, not an ideology', identifying its key features as emotionalisation and over-simplification of highly complex issues such as Brexit, the COVID pandemic and migration. She pointed out the reliance of demagogues on bogeymen. Populists, she said, depend on enemies, real or imagined, to legitimise their actions and divert attention from their own shortcomings.

After the Brexit vote, former Chancellor of the Exchequer Philip Hammond, the Labour Party and Prime Minister Boris Johnson's sister Rachel – none of them conspiracy theorists with mad staring eyes – all suggested that the government's plan to sign off Brexit by the end of October, whether or not there was a 'deal', was part of a conspiracy with hedge-fund financiers who would earn billions if Britain crashed out of the European Union. This was no surprise: there's always a lurking conspiracy theory about pesky hedge-fund managers. The question to ask is, though: how would we know it was true? Where should we look for the evidence?

Indeed, what evidence would you need to demonstrate that any of these conspiracy theories was false? Because if there is no way to show that a theory (or, more strictly, a hypothesis) is false, it doesn't really deserve to be called a theory. After all, there is a theory that every Christmas Eve Father Christmas delivers presents to every child in the world by entering their house down the chimney. The evidence for this is worse than feeble: the whole idea is physically impossible. Yet there isn't a person who has managed to prove that the theory is false. I am reserving judgement.

Watergate

'Conspiracy theorist' is often a weapon-phrase designed to damage whoever is on the receiving end of it. Many people who suggest that some secretive influential organisation is conspiring in an illegal event find this loaded term pointed at them. From time to time, however, a lurid and unlikely-sounding conspiracy theory turns out to be true, quickly becomes part of the historical record and is put on the National Curriculum. At this point the term 'conspiracy theory' is quietly dropped and the wild-eyed conspiracy theorist becomes just another historian.

This is what happened with the ridiculous idea that the Earth orbited the Sun, not the other way around, and also with the infamous Watergate affair, a series of over-lapping political scandals in the early seventies, which led to the self-destruction of President Richard Nixon. This is how the business unfolded.

Sometime after midnight on Saturday, 17 June 1972, at the Watergate Complex, a group of apartment and office buildings in the Foggy Bottom area of Washington, DC, a security guard noticed that latches on some of the office doors of the Democratic National Committee campaign headquarters had been taped open, preventing them from locking. Although he didn't yet know it, a gang of burglars were in the office and were about to accidentally pull on the thread that would unravel the Nixon presidency. In any case, the guard called the police, and three passing plainclothes officers dressed as hippies entered the building.

In a room in the Howard Johnson motel over the road, the burglars' lookout saw the long-haired cops in their flares walking up the stairwell steps and radioed a warning. But in a classic piece of uselessness, the burglars had turned off their walkie-talkie, and the lookout was unable to tip them off. The police captured five men and their tools: lock-picks, crowbars, two 35mm cameras, a short-wave receiver and three tear-gas guns.

The burglars were: Bernard Barker, Virgilio Gonzalez, Rolando Eugenio Martinez and Frank Sturgis (born Frank Fiorini), all part-Cuban anti-Castro activists recruited by a CIA agent named E. Howard Hunt, a former White House consultant. The fifth, James W. McCord, was a former CIA and FBI agent, and a security consultant on Nixon's campaign staff. These men were used to 'back-bag' work of this kind. Some, like Sturgis/ Fiorini, had been involved in the CIA's Bay of Pigs invasion fiasco. Sturgis had also recruited Fidel Castro's young girlfriend Marita Lorenz in a CIA-planned attempt on his life. Lorenz said she met Sturgis once more in 1963, just before the Kennedy assassination (*see page 18*), when she drove to Dallas with him and a group of anti-Castro militants including E. Howard Hunt. They told her they were involved in setting up 'something big';

she did not know what. Intriguingly, Sturgis's secret FBI file is, according to muckrock.com, 75,253 pages long, almost twice the length of the FBI's Watergate and Kennedy assassination files put together.

In January 1973, the five burglars were convicted of conspiracy, burglary and violation of federal wiretapping laws. Also charged were E. Howard Hunt and G. Gordon Liddy, a former FBI agent and member of the White House staff, who were said to be the brains behind the Watergate burglary.

Coverage by *Washington Post* reporters Bob Woodward and Carl Bernstein revealed that evidence of knowledge of the break-in and attempts to cover it up lurked in the bowels of the Justice Department, the FBI, the CIA and, crucially, Nixon's White House. Woodward and Bernstein said the Watergate break-in was part of a huge campaign of political spying and sabotage linked to the official Committee to Re-elect the President (CREEP). Despite their front-page revelations of this vast conspiracy at the heart of government, the president was re-elected in a huge November landslide.

But the reporters had an excellent source, nicknamed 'Deep Throat' in honour of a porn film of that name. When Woodward wanted to meet Deep Throat, he would put a flowerpot containing a red flag on his apartment balcony. Later he would find his copy of the *New York Times* on the step, with a little clock drawn in on one page, signalling a meeting time in the early hours. These encounters took place in an unromantic underground car park in Washington. Here, Deep Throat told Woodward that he and Bernstein were onto something really significant: Nixon's senior aides had paid the burglars to illegally dig up information about the president's political opponents. Deep Throat also tipped off Woodward to Howard Hunt's involvement, and warned him that he might be followed and that his phone might be bugged. It was all rather thrilling.

A Senate Watergate Committee formed to investigate the scandal discovered that President Nixon had long been tape recording his office conversations. These very sweary tapes implicated him in the cover-up and showed that he was well aware of what the five burglars and their associates had been up to.

Nixon's press secretary dodged accusations of impeachable malpractice by describing the Watergate break-in as 'a third-rate burglary attempt', but after two years of denial, and endless claims by the administration of 'wild accusations' and a conspiracy theory gone mad, Nixon's own lawyers realised that the president had been repeatedly lying to the people, to his closest aides and to them. Faced with imminent impeachment, Nixon decided to jump before he was pushed, and on 9 August 1974 he grudgingly resigned, the only US president ever to do so.

The Watergate scandal resulted in sixty-nine government officials being charged and forty-eight being found guilty. At that point, talk of wild accusations and conspiracy theories simply evaporated and everyone said how regrettable the whole thing had been. Nixon was pardoned by the new president, Gerald Ford.

Black Helicopters

Linked with Men in Black and kindred conspiracy theories, black helicopters are said to be signs of a forthcoming military takeover, or planned United Nations invasion of the USA. The first black helicopter stories took off in the 1970s and were linked to reported incidents of cattle mutilation and UFO sightings. These mysterious aircraft are still part of a vibrant conspiracy theory and are said to be invisible to radar and able to fly in ways that normal choppers cannot. They belong, it is claimed, to a secret government department whose job is to hide from the public all evidence of alien stopovers on Earth. Black helicopter stories have now spread via social media out beyond the US and into international airspace.

On 23 January 2020, 'official advice' began circulating in Wuhan, the Chinese city at the centre of the COVID-19 outbreak, that 'Navy airplanes' would be spraying disinfectant over the area and that people should stay at home and wash any food they had bought from street traders. As the rumour spread on social media, 'airplanes' soon became 'helicopters'.

The incoherence of the 'warning' that the authorities were 'protecting' the public by spraying a dangerous substance failed to stop the gossip and Chinese officials were obliged to issue repeated denials. But mud sticks and the more they denied it the more suspicious it sounded. 'Helicopters' quickly became 'black helicopters' and within a few short months a fully-fledged conspiracy theory had taken wing.

By March, Spain, Russia, India, Switzerland, the USA and Canada – along with several other countries – were reporting the same claims. People were being 'advised' to stay indoors and keep windows closed. Very few seemed bothered that the source for this 'advice' and the conspiracy theory that had grown out of it was not the government but social media.

This particular theory seems to have predated the virus outbreak, beginning in September 2019 during pro-democracy protests in Hong Kong, during which helicopters were said to have sprayed protestors with a fluorescent powder, rendering them feeble and obedient. While the internet was full of these menacing black helicopters, reputable sources were not.

The word 'helicopter' is made from two other words, divided not like this: *heli* and *copter*; but like this: *helico* and *pter*, from the Greek *helix*, 'spiral', and *pteron*, 'wing'. The first *black* helicopter stories appeared when Air America was running test flights of two black Hughes Aircraft Company helicopters in California, in the 1970s. Air America was in fact a dummy passenger airline secretly owned by the CIA and run as a private commercial company between 1950 and 1976, before it was wound up and the name taken by a real passenger airline.

Around the same time, author Hal Lindsey suggested in his book *The Late, Great Planet Earth* that the ravening locusts referred to in the Book of Revelation were in reality helicopters, though, unlike Air America, his hard-to-disprove theory failed to take off.

Other theories have been more popular, including one which says that the US government, conspiring with the United Nations, has prepared fleets of black helicopters ready for military occupation of America when the New World Order (*see page 149*) comes to pass. The trouble with this theory was that, though it attracted some interest at the time, it also attracted ridicule enough that the term 'black helicopters' was soon being used as a shorthand for the loopiest conspiracy theories.

But this did nothing to stop black helicopter sightings over town and country alike. Men in Black (*see page 33*) are sometimes said to descend from the helicopters, waving guns, and in at least one instance they were reported to have climbed down a rudimentary rope ladder. This doesn't sound very cool; you would have thought such sophisticated craft would be equipped with a decent set of steps.

A fairly recent sighting was written up in American newspapers, which quoted an unnamed woman explaining exactly what she and her husband had seen: 'My husband is a long-haul truck driver and we were on a run from Washington State to Albuquerque … I spotted three glowing objects to the west over the hills. My husband pulled over and we observed the objects … The next day outside Boulder City, Nevada, at about 6 a.m. we videoed fifteen black helicopters flying in the direction of where we saw the objects the night before.'

Unfortunately, this report does not stand up to very close scrutiny. The photographs do show dark helicopters, but as they have been snapped against the bright sky their sombre tone is hardly surprising. Indeed, helicopters in flight generally look black when photographed from below. The motionless 'UFOs' themselves look pretty much like cloudlets or lens flares caused by the low sun – a common photographic aberration.

All the same, we now know that the US government has indeed developed black stealth helicopters, but it's the technology that is secret, not the helicopters themselves. Along with the FBI, the immigration and drug enforcement agencies use such aircraft, and US Customs and Border Protection reportedly has a dozen Black Hawks. In fact, their presence was long ago admitted by the then US commander in chief, President Barack Obama. 'There are black helicopters,' he remarked, 'but we generally don't deploy them on US soil.' That 'generally' is interesting. But as with some other conspiracy theories, the mystery around their routine use has set a hare running, so that the frequent sighting of everyday surveillance or narcotics patrols causes febrile reports of strange goings-on.

The claims that black helicopters are equipped with a silent 'stealth' mode and can do all kinds of things that ordinary choppers cannot do turn out to be true. Stealth technology includes infrared-heat suppression systems and special stealthy fuselage construction, as well as highly developed composite airframe materials that reduce radar presence.

One helicopter developed by the US in the late nineties was 360 times less detectible by radar, and apparently six times quieter. In 2011, two 'stealthed' Black Hawks, modified to minimise heat, noise and radar signature, were used in the US killing of Osama bin Laden. Latest developments include something referred to enigmatically as a 'digital camouflage system', and similar research continues, so it is claimed, at Area 51 (*see page 37*).

Of course, all this is ultimately run by the government. In his first military briefing, sometime President Donald Trump was told that a black helicopter had crashed and killed two Brazilian people. 'Goddammit!' he yelled. 'How many is a brazilian?'

VIII

WHO'S PULLING THE STRINGS?

Secret Societies that Run the World

We are easily fooled by that
which we love.

—MOLIÈRE

The Bilderberg Group

Every year a secretive group of the world's most power-ful heads of state, politicians, royalty, giants of commerce, finance, media and industry convene at a luxury hotel somewhere in the rich world. Known as 'the Bilderberg Group', after the hotel where they first met, in 1954, this so-called 'cabal' get together to exchange ideas out of the public gaze. There is a different guest list each year, with anything from 120 to 150 people, and security is tight. Heavily armed guards roam the area. Membership of the group is by invitation only, and most members are invited only once or twice. The aims of the Bilderberg Group – it is claimed – include the abolition of nation-states, global military control, the imposition of a single currency, the concentration of wealth in the hands of the select few and, naturally enough, world domination.

The Bilderberg Group was established by Polish poli-tician and power broker Józef Retinger, who decided to coordinate post-war anti-communist resistance by 'fostering dialogue' between Europe and North America. The first thing he did to create an unofficial 'working group' of world leaders was to have a word with the Dutch Prince Bernhard of Lippe-Biesterfeld. He also bent the ear of the then head of Unilever, Paul Rijkens, and the Belgian prime minister, Paul van Zeeland, a founder of the European League for Economic Cooperation.

These heavyweights invited other European and US leaders into their new group, along with figures from industry, academia, the media and finance. At least fifty delegates from eleven European countries turned up to the first meeting, along with eleven Americans. Since then, there has been about one Bilderberg meeting a year.

The first US conference was held in 1957, sponsored by the Ford Foundation to the tune of $30,000. Heinz are among past donors, along with Barclays, Daimler, Fiat, IBM, GlaxoSmithKline, Nokia and Royal Dutch Shell, who all presumably believe the decisions being made will be in their interests.

Discussions are 'informal' and revolve around 'megatrends', but rumours abound that unattributable commands are issued at meetings, before the appointees return home to implement them. NATO General Secretary Willy Claes, who turned up for the 1994 meeting, said that each 'delegate' is supposed to apply the meetings' various conclusions to 'his circle of influence'.

Members of the Bilderberg Group are certainly in the right position to influence global affairs, having unbeatable political, media and financial connections. They claim to be 'a diverse group', yet three-quarters of them are rich men, the rest rich women. They boast of their transparency, but no minutes are published, there is no voting and nothing is formally resolved. The lack of published minutes, they claim, is to preserve anonymity and allow free expression of ideas: just the atmosphere you need for shady 'back-room' deals and influence peddling.

Because of the high profile of the guests, and the very low profile of what actually goes on behind closed doors, the field is ripe for conspiracy theories, with the Left and Right each having their own preferred ideas.

Those on the left claim that Bilderberg Group members are conspiring to stamp free-market capitalist tyranny on the world, while those on the right allege a plot to impose one world government and, horror of horrors, a planned economy. The right-wing John Birch Society and conspiracy theorist Alex Jones (*see page 49*) are to be found stating their Bilderberg beliefs in their usual moderate style, while David Icke (*see page 192*) says the Bilderbergers are a potentially satanic cabal of shape-shifting lizards that are doing the work of the Illuminati (*see page 187*), controlling everything, and are out to enslave the entire human race. He may be going a bit far there.

In 2006 Lithuanian-born conspiracy theorist Daniel Estulin published *The True Story of the Bilderberg Group*, which suggested that the clique was indeed planning world domination. In 2010, sometime Cuban president Fidel Castro wrote a 'reflection' on this book, praising Estulin, and quoting him on the subject of 'a world government that knows no borders and is not accountable to anyone but its own self'. The Bilderberg people are no doubt delighted to count the late Fidel Castro as a critic.

All the same, many do question the group's secretive transnational lobbying and there is a school which maintains that the post-war push for a united Europe actually springs from the Bilderbergers. Founder member, Labour Party Deputy Leader Denis Healey, explained: 'To say we were striving for a one world government is exaggerated, but not wholly unfair,' though he meant this in the sense of the global struggle to put a stop to the grim history of European wars, destruction, homelessness and death.

The Bilderberg Group has been accused of the 'heavy-handed' treatment of journalists, and one does wonder why they are getting so jumpy about the press. In 2017, journalist Charlie Skelton, who has been reporting on the Bilderberg Group for more than a decade, wrote in the *Guardian* that an agenda item for that year's meeting was 'The war on information'. He wondered which side of this 'war' the world's most secretive conference was on, the Bilderbergers having spent 'hundreds of thousands of dollars' keeping the press away. He explained that he had many times been 'bundled into police cars and yelled at to hand over my camera' while trying to report on the conference, or been escorted from his bedroom in the early hours and ordered to stand under a police spotlight. None of this is going to make the man or woman in the street warm to the Bilderberg Group, and it only pours fuel onto the conspiracy-theory fire.

The presence of media bosses at Bilderberg meetings makes the secrecy look even odder. What reputable journalist would agree not to report what he or she sees? In an Orwellian breath of scorn from the horse's mouth, Bilderberg insider Richard Salant, sometime president of CBS News, said of the media's role: 'Our job is not to give people what they want, but what we decide they should have.'

The Masons

Of the men I've met over the years who have let slip that they are Masons, most are not what you'd imagine when you hear seductive theories about their supposedly sinister order. They tend to be the managing directors of local cardboard-box factories, dressed in polyester suits and ties, or pot-bellied police constables, who tell bad jokes at the golf club and like the idea of putting on a funny apron and rolling up their trouser leg of an evening.

When it began, in the Middle Ages, Freemasonry was a loose collection of mild-mannered fraternal organisations of European, English and Scottish stonemasons. By the time of the signing of the US Constitution, however, it had become a significant power in the United States. Several founding fathers were Freemasons, including George Washington and Benjamin Franklin, and by the twentieth century the Masons could count among their most senior officials members of the British royal family. Along with growing influence went the flavour of secrecy, and as with all secret societies, such as MI6 and the Brownies, mystery led to doubt, doubt to curiosity, curiosity to gossip, and gossip, finally, to conspiracy theories.

In the early hours of the morning of 12 September 1826, New York stoneworker William Morgan suddenly disappeared. Morgan had inveigled his way into the secret society of the Freemasons and, after a bit, started telling all and sundry that he was about to publish a sensational exposé of the 'strongest evidence of rottenness' in the Masons' arcane rituals and initiation ceremonies.

Hoping to stop the book's publication, a group of boozed-up local Masons went about things in the simplest way, and set fire to the print works. They then arranged for Morgan's arrest by officers with masonic links and bent noses. These men turned up at his house waving an arrest warrant for an outstanding debt of $2.65. Morgan was held only briefly before his bail was paid, highly suspiciously, by the Masons themselves. On release he was manhandled into a carriage before being galloped away, never to be seen again.

When caught, the rascals accused of William Morgan's disappearance were given only light sentences and it looked as if the secretive, hierarchical and influential Masons had got their chums off lightly. But the plan failed to work, and, as usually happens, the attempt to hush up a book actually turned it into a bestseller. The publicity also caused a change from major to minor in the national mood-music, so that Freemasonry became an emblem for all America's perceived, and actual, faults. The Anti-Masonic Party was suddenly a national force, causing a fall-off in the organisation's membership, a loss of masonic influence across the nation and a gradual rise in masonic conspiracy theorising.

Hundreds of these theories have surfaced since the eighteenth century, covering everything from allegations of Freemasons exerting control over government, to religious and occult antics. In modern times, the Masons were said to have faked the Apollo Moon landings (*see page 116*), and hidden the fact that the Earth is flat (*see page 111*).

Like other secretive organisations they are a useful target for pointing fingers after something like the death of Princess Diana (*see page 3*). As early as 1792, theories had emerged linking Freemasonry, the Illuminati, the Knights Templar and the usual religious suspects with a plan for universal control of governments and financial institutions, and the creation of a New World Order (*see page 149*).

The British judiciary, we are told, is full of Masons, just like the police force; and when a judge feels his intuition telling him that the chap sitting in the dock for fiddling his accounts is a fellow Mason he lets him off lightly. Quite how a judge knows a masonic fellow traveller from an ordinary criminal I'm not sure. Judges are not in the habit of popping down the cells in their red dressing gown and horsehair wig to try out the old masonic handshake on East-End ne'er-do-wells.

Freemasonry is said to be an occult practice, worshiping a God named GAOTU: The Great Architect of the Universe, or, some have claimed, Satan. In their defence, the Masons point out that Lodge meetings contain no worship, and discussion of religion is forbidden. Freemasonry, they protest, is a 'progressive science', and the confusion with religion comes from rituals and symbols, which may look like those of organised religion. Paradoxically, though, they say that one requirement for membership is belief in 'a higher spiritual being'.

OK, let's have a look at all that. First, no science, 'progressive' or otherwise, would forbid discussion of religion, or anything. Indeed, scientists are often enthusiastic in their willingness to debate such subjects. Second, you could be forgiven for thinking that the requirement to believe in 'a higher spiritual being' is identical in sense to the first definition of 'religion' in Oxford's online dictionary: 'The belief in and worship of a superhuman controlling power, especially a personal God or gods.' So, score so far: conspiracy theorists – 1; Freemasonry – a big fat 0.

As well as the major masonic conspiracy theories there is also a quirkier one, which claims that masonic symbols have long been hidden under our very noses. The most interesting example is the 'All-seeing Eye', which you can find on the back of the dollar bill, floating inside a triangle above an unfinished pyramid. This emblem is second only in importance to the Masons' square and compasses, and is said to have been on the dollar from its earliest days.

In fact, that idea is incorrect. The Eye of Providence, shown inside a triangle with sun rays, was not added to the currency until 1935 and was intended as a symbol of the Christian deity watching benevolently over humanity. It first appeared on the Great Seal of the United States in 1782 but wasn't adopted by the Freemasons for another fifteen years, and then without the triangle, but with a cloud.

At the root of all these conspiracy theories is the Masons' own insistence on secrecy, so they can hardly complain. But many do, objecting that the endless carping about their supposedly malevolent intentions ignores all their charitable support for the Red Cross, and children's homes, and other good works, which, they say, are taken for granite.

The Illuminati

Lurking in the shadows behind almost every major global event of the past few centuries stands a highly secret group of powerful men pulling the strings. Their plan: to establish a master race and set up a New World Order. Their name: 'the Illuminati'. That's what people say, anyway.

The Illuminati are not new. The organisation was founded in 1776 as a secret society of Bavarian intellectuals, whose goals were quite different from the Illuminati of today. The first Illuminati aimed to put an end to 'the machinations of the purveyors of injustice', to counter superstition, fight the abuses of state power, stay the oppressive hand of religion in the lives of ordinary people and promote the ideas of the Enlightenment. Hence their appellation, which comes from the Latin *illuminatus*, meaning 'enlightened'.

Nonetheless, as with the Freemasons (*see page 182*), the Illuminati were a thorn in the side of the powerful. So with the backing of the Catholic Church the government rapidly made them illegal. But in their absence paranoia thrived and the bush telegraph was soon alive with the news that the organisation had gone underground. Before you could say 'unfounded rumour' it was common knowledge that the Illuminati were behind the French Revolution (1789–1799).

This, though, was just the start. From such reliable sources as Facebook we now learn that during the Battle of Waterloo it was the Illuminati who were pulling the levers. They were at the root of the First and Second World Wars, the Great Depression, the Korean and Vietnam Wars, the assassination of JFK and the collapse of Soviet communism. The Illuminati are, it seems, also responsible for the 2002 SARS virus, the 2009 H1N1 virus, COVID-19 and the murder of John Lennon, though quite what that one did for them is a bit of a puzzle. Looking at all this, it strikes me that the Illuminati conspiracy theory is the conspiracy theory to top all conspiracy theories.

The group can, apparently, trace its origins at least as far back as the Knights Templar (*see page 80*), who were, apparently, the secret society in embryonic form. Descended from thirteen interrelated families whose bloodline now reaches into every cranny of political and industrial power and influence, the modern Illuminati, it is claimed, mastermind world events by infiltrating their own kind into government and big business so as to establish a feudal state in which the 'middle class' is to be abolished in favour of a society of medieval-style rulers and serfs.

Already they have secured their foothold. Most industrialists, bankers and world leaders conspire with this sinister world power, or so it is claimed. Prominent politicians, corporate elites, oil men, big pharma, the aristocracy, the presidents of the United States and the British royals are all said to be members of the Illuminati. Even Hollywood and the media have been infiltrated and the Illuminati crop up in films and books aplenty, including *Angels & Demons* (2009), Hollywood's sequel to *The Da Vinci Code*.

The globalisation the world has seen so far is only the first step on the road to one world government. In this New World Order, national and regional borders will be abolished and a single world currency established, along with a unified military. Finally, because a large population threatens survival and a small population is easier to control, the Illuminati will wipe most of us out as they bring global numbers down from about eight billion to one billion people. Only the acquiescent will survive. Those who protest will be exterminated, though working out where to bury seven billion dead bodies is going to be some headache.

But where did these ideas spring from?

Digging around a bit, I discovered that, rather like the 'Avril Lavigne is dead' conspiracy theory (*see page 54*), the Illuminati business started with a prank: a playful hippy hoax launched at the height of flower power, during the Summer of Love.

Robert Edward Wilson (pen name Robert Anton Wilson), a druggy American ambulance driver and writer, decided, together with his pot-raddled buddy Kerry Thornley, to shake the authoritarian world up a bit. To start, they sent fake readers' letters into *Playboy* magazine, where Wilson was an editor, mentioning a secret organisation of elites, known as the Illuminati. Next they sent in 'replies', contradicting their own original letters. The idea was that the conflicting views would cause readers to ask themselves, 'Hey, can I trust the way information is being presented to me?' This sceptical analysis would then spread to the population at large.

The second weapon in their struggle against authority was a jokey, quasi-religious leaflet that set out the precepts of Discordianism, a 'faith' dreamt up by Kerry Thornley and Greg Hill, a beardy computer nerd. Their hope was that by poking authority in the eye with five scrappy copies of their pamphlet *Principia Discordia, or How I Found Goddess and What I Did to Her When I Found Her* they would bring about fundamental social change. Robert Anton Wilson, co-author of the fake *Playboy* letters, quoted it extensively in *The Illuminatus! Trilogy*, a spoof he wrote with Robert Shea, another *Playboy* editor. This title blamed modern conspiracies and cover-ups on their invented group, the Illuminati.

The Illuminatus! Trilogy became a cult success. When it was put on in the seventies as a ten-hour stage play at the National Theatre it launched the careers of both Jim Broadbent and Bill Nighy. A role-play game then appeared, infecting a whole generation with the delusion that the Illuminati were a real and pressing danger.

All that psychedelic tobacco seems to have fuzzed the minds of Messrs Wilson and Thornley, who rather over-estimated the analytical competence of *Playboy*'s readers, and the hoped-for realisation among rational readers and theatregoers that the whole thing was a spoof failed to happen. Instead, the rumours began to grow, and within a few short years social media had got its hands on the Illuminati conspiracy theory, creating an unstoppable tsunami of twaddle.

Ickeonography

The Lizardy World of David Icke

David Icke is a sometime footballer and sports reporter, who in 1983 co-hosted *Grandstand*, the BBC's longest-running TV sports programme. He then became a politician, before evolving into a professional conspiracy theorist with a worldwide following of readers and viewers.

Icke explained that in the late eighties he had begun to feel a 'presence' around him and was so bothered by it in a hotel room one day in 1990 that he asked: 'If there is anybody here, will you please contact me because you are driving me up the wall?' A few days later, on the Isle of Wight, he felt his feet being attracted to the ground by a 'force', and a voice in his head led him towards a book called *Mind to Mind* by a psychic healer named Betty Shine.

Icke, who has bad arthritis, asked Shine for a consultation. After several visits he felt something like a spider's web on his face and Shine told him he had been sent to 'heal the Earth'. Having done a bit of channelling, Icke received, through automatic writing, the message that he was a 'Son of the Godhead', and then underwent what he called his 'turquoise period', rather like Picasso. He began to wear a turquoise shell suit because he thought this was the best colour for a positive-energy conduit. The trouble was that turquoise wasn't really his shade and he soon dropped it. Anyway, he announced that the world was going to end in 1997, signalled by an earthquake on the Isle of Arran. Nobody took much notice, and after 1 January 1998 he stopped talking about this so much.

None of these ideas was what you would call a conspiracy theory, but in his book *The Biggest Secret* (1999) Icke broached his main conspiracy idea: that several public figures were actually reptilian humanoids descended from the Anunnaki, giant deities in horned caps who came from a distant constellation called Draco (Latin for 'dragon').

Over time this lizard-people hypothesis evolved, and the essence of it now is that demonic reptilians, known as the Archons, once 'hijacked' the Earth, and while they were about it they cross-bred with human women to produce a mixed-race Archon/human bloodline of shape-shifting lizardy types, known as the 'Babylonian Brotherhood', who live in caverns inside the Earth.

Icke said he believed the entire universe to be made up of 'vibrational energy' and that humans are being manipulated to keep them from realising this. Nowadays, apparently with some sort of support from the London School of Economics, the Lizard Men control the United Nations, the International Monetary Fund and the Bilderberg Group (*see page 177*), as well as the media, the military, Western spy organisations, the internet, religion and science. Icke incidentally describes science as 'bollocks', an attitude you can understand, coming from him, though as science was behind the development of the internet, where he preaches his gospel, the material his shell suits were made of and research into helping people with arthritis, like him, I don't think he should be quite so dismissive.

The Lizard Men, Icke believes, keep humans fearful and hatred-filled by engaging in paedophilia and cannibalism, and by manipulating world events. They feed off the resulting 'negative energy', which does at least sound low calorie. Their grand aim is to microchip the population and set up a fascist New World Order. 'Thus we have,' he wrote, 'the mass slaughter of animals, sexual perversions which create highly charged negative energy, and black magic ritual and sacrifice which takes place on a scale that will stagger those who have not studied the subject.'

This sensational conspiracy theory quickly attracted certain people, though others asked themselves what evidence there might be for it all. Icke explained: 'From 1998, I started coming across people who told me they had seen people change into a non-human form. It's an age-old phenomenon known as shape-shifting. The basic form is like a scaly humanoid, with reptilian rather than humanoid eyes.'

Obviously, Dave couldn't tell us who these people were who told him they had seen this, but he did offer the evidence of his own experience. He explained that in 1989, while waiting with former British Prime Minister Sir Edward Heath to be interviewed for television, he saw Ted's eyes go completely 'jet black'.

But Heath was small beer. In 2016 Icke told interviewer Andrew Neil that the British royal family are all shape-shifting lizards. Now, Prince Andrew you could understand, but all of them? He had even remarked that the Queen Mother was 'seriously reptilian'. Rather tactless, you might think, seeing as she was 101 at the time he said it. The Lizard Men, he suggests, are the modern edition of the old-time reptile-Aryan 'royalty', though the reptile lineage also includes British prime ministers, a smattering of celebrities, including Bob Hope, and all the American presidents.

All this you could accept, or not, and not much harm would have been done. But, in April 2020, Icke claimed in an interview posted on YouTube that 5G mobile-phone networks were somehow connected to the COVID-19 pandemic (*see page 136*), and that requiring people to be vaccinated against COVID-19 amounted to 'fascism'. 'If 5G continues and reaches where they want to take it,' he said, 'human life as we know it is over …' About this time, a number of mobile-phone masts were deliberately set on fire, and telecom engineers were menaced. British media regulator Ofcom said that Icke's opinions 'had the potential to cause significant harm to viewers' and 'were made without the support of any scientific or other evidence'. On 1 May 2020 Facebook took down his main page, and the next day YouTube removed the Icke interview in question.

You know, I sometimes worry about old Ickey. He acknowledges that it was at a time of personal despair that he began to feel the 'presence' around him, and in

2001 he told Jon Ronson: 'As a television presenter, I'd been respected. People come up to you in the street and shake your hand and talk to you in a respectful way.' That sounds like someone very needy for positive attention. Do his conspiracy theories provide another way of meeting that need? I haven't a clue, but I hope he's OK.

IX

THE X FILES

The Weirdest of All Conspiracies

A deception that elevates us is dearer
than a host of low truths.

—ALEKSANDR PUSHKIN

QAnon

QAnon is a far-right conspiracy theory that began with a supposed secret plot by the 'deep state' against President Donald Trump and his supporters. QAnon started in 2017 with a post on the anonymous imageboard 4chan by a mysterious figure calling himself, or herself, 'Q'. Like a biblical prophet, Q foretold of significant events to come, such as the 'Great Awakening' and the less meta-physical forthcoming arrest of Hillary Clinton, an event that, as it turned out, never happened.

QAnon sprang from the 2016 'Pizzagate' conspiracy theory, which baselessly claimed that Clinton was running a paedophile ring in the basement of a pizzeria called Comet Ping Pong (*see page 210*). The movement is backed by an improbable congregation that includes wellness groups, vigilante 'paedophile hunter' networks, pro-Brexit campaigners, older conspiracy forums and far-right extremists. Though it started in the USA, QAnon is growing in popularity across other countries. In October 2020 the UK press reported that a quarter of Britons believed in QAnon-linked theories, such as secretive powerful elites in Hollywood, politics and the media engaging in child-trafficking. In Britain, more than a third of youngsters between the ages of eighteen and twenty-four said they believed such implausible stories.

QAnon was just made for social media, and Twitter is its natural home. With its limits on character count Twitter is the ideal place for people who want short, simple answers to complex questions. QAnon has a vast number of Twitter fans, and the *Guardian* found more than 170 QAnon groups, pages and accounts on Facebook and Instagram, with 4.5 million aggregate followers, who commonly tag their social media posts with the hashtag #WWG1WGA, signifying the syntactically weird motto 'Where We Go One, We Go All'. This phrase is borrowed from the film *White Squall* (1996), a sentimental disaster-survival film that Q seems keen on. There is also a healthy business in online merchandise, including a reviving beverage called 'Great Awakening coffee'.

Together with quasi-paranoid tales of left-wing sex abuse and cannibalism, the pet topics of QAnon's followers include the belief that COVID-19 might have been faked by the 'deep state'. In 2020 QAnon spread news that President Trump's wearing of a yellow tie at a White House briefing secretly signalled that the virus threat was fake, because the tie was, as one QAnon superspreader ungrammatically put it, 'the exact same color as the maritime flag that represents the vessel has no infected people on board'. I spent a happy half-hour looking up international maritime flags and discovered that the yellow one actually means 'I request free pratique', which is a licence to enter port.

In 2020, sites spreading health misinformation got about half a billion views on Facebook in just one month. A report by campaign group Avaaz found that the top ten sites publishing false information and health conspiracy theories were viewed nearly four times as often on Facebook as the top ten sites publishing accurate information. Writing in the *American Journal of Tropical Medicine and Hygiene*, researchers directly linked 800 deaths to a single piece of COVID-19 misinformation.

QAnon has posted various plugs for other conspiracy theories for which evidence is thin on the ground, including the claim that a named politician had sexually molested a boy's corpse at a hotel, and another suggesting that Michelle Obama is a man.

President Trump was himself keen on retweeting QAnon's posts and in 2020 said he was glad to have support from QAnon-supporting voters. And it wasn't just voters: in the US presidential election that year, Republican Marjorie Taylor Greene became the first QAnon supporter to win a seat in the House.

All this QAnon stuff is a bit cheesy, and though some of it is harmless claptrap, some of it isn't. The FBI has warned that fringe conspiracy theories such as QAnon are a domestic terrorism threat, and political science professor Joe Uscinski, who is an expert on conspiracy theories, describes QAnon beliefs as almost an incitement to violence. 'I mean, there isn't anything worse you can say about your political competitors than that they are satanic sex traffickers who molest and eat children.'

The involvement of QAnon supporters in the invasion of the US Capitol in January 2021 is a good example of their power. Inflamed by their president's rhetoric, a mob of hooligans, some flourishing QAnon placards, others armed with napalm-like Molotov cocktails, guns, bullets and explosive devices, broke into the building and a police officer died in the line of duty, defending the place and the people working inside it. As Voltaire said, 'Those who can make you believe absurdities can make you commit atrocities.' This is when conspiracy theories stop being funny.

As people have begun to wake up to what is happening, some internet platforms have started to take action. Facebook, YouTube and TikTok all restricted QAnon content, and in July 2020 Twitter banned thousands of QAnon-affiliated accounts, citing 'clear and well-documented informational, physical, societal and psychological offline harm'. Shortly after the violent 2021 insurrection, Twitter and Facebook both booted Donald Trump off their platforms. This is an ongoing problem for social media providers.

In the *New York Times*, columnist Kevin Roose suggested that many social media users have absorbed a worldview centred on YouTube and Facebook, rejecting reliable television networks, reputable journals and journalists, and properly researched books, calling them 'fake'. There seems to be a newly prevalent inability among people to understand how to test the probable truth or falsity of a proposition. But one thing's for sure: a seductively outlandish post on an anonymous internet 'imageboard' is not a reliable source. Neither are offbeat online 'authorities' with 'secret knowledge' and conspiratorial explanations unsupported by evidence.

There is a tendency for those who make such claims to hide behind pseudonyms, usernames and anonymity. There is doubtless a great satisfaction in doing it this way, since it endows posters with the power to say what they like, with no comeback. Some of the people who do this appear to be operating from a very low level of mental health.

The abandonment of reason and disinterested objectivity in favour of credulity and emotion resembles the burgeoning of a new cult or religion. Religious parallels are notable with QAnon. These include ideas of reincarnation, a metaphysics beyond our understanding and a mysterious omniscient power whose real name we must not utter. In return, those who believe and belong receive privileged warnings of a great catastrophe, and the promise of a better time to come.

QAnon's followers seem to like being part of this community of privileged knowers: there is a palpable feeling of belonging, and a sense of Them and Us. The language and flavour of evangelical Christianity abound, with a peppering of portentous asides such as 'Nothing can stop what is coming' or 'Some things must remain classified to the very end'.

In an article in *The Atlantic*, Adrienne LaFrance pointed out that QAnon's fans speak of their leader, 'Q', in quasi-religious terms. They describe a sense of rebirth, and know a 'Great Awakening' is coming. In September 2020, however, a hole was blown in this numinous mystery by the revelation that there were connections to moneymaking. Fact-checking news site Logically unmasked forty-eight-year-old Jason Gelinas as the operator of QMap, a website that organised Q's postings. A senior vice president of American multinational investment bank Citigroup, and an experienced IT expert, Gelinas was reportedly bringing in more than $3,000 a month from his Q activities, with the *New York Post* saying he looked like 'a major player in the secretive QAnon structure'. He told Bloomberg that QAnon was 'a patriotic movement to save the country'. He was put on leave.

As with the assertions of Scientology or Christianity, or indeed any religion, the enigmatic claims of QAnon cannot be confirmed or falsified. If you ask, 'Is there proof that babies and children are being secretly tortured and raped by left-wing members of the deep state?' you are likely to be met with the response: 'Well, is there any evidence they're not?' The answer to this is: 'No, but that doesn't mean we should all start believing it's true.'

Fake Finland

Finland is a Nordic European country with a snowy population of five and a half million, about two million fewer than London. Up the top, next to Norway, sits Finnish Lapland, with its twinkling pine forests, horny-antlered reindeer and Father Christmas. Near Finland's bottom lies the Baltic Sea, home to the notorious Baltic herring, which, when fermented, gives off a perfume so extraordinary it makes people vomit as they open the can. The country is also renowned for its delicious ammonium chloride liquorice, its northern lights, its islands, lakes and saunas.

At least this is what we are led to believe, and as we approach Helsinki Airport out of a cold blue sky, it certainly appears that way. But what you might not know as your plane touches down is that there is no such place as Finland, and that the whole apparition is a giant international conspiracy.

The Finland conspiracy theory says that the area we think of as Finland is really just a lot of sea, and that Japan has conspired with Russia to get the world to agree that there is actually a country there, so as to conceal their secret overfishing of the area. To keep everyone believing in this mirage, maps have been stealthily redrawn. When business people and tourists land in Helsinki they are actually arriving in a bit of eastern Sweden, and since one Nordic forest looks very much like another, who's to know the difference?

The history of this story goes like this. After the Second World War Japan had overfished its waters and needed somewhere new to catch fish. So they suggested to the Russians, who were very short of food, that Russia should give them secret rights to catch herring in the Baltic Sea in exchange for a bit of the catch, and the two countries would conceal this agreement from the world.

The easiest and cheapest way to do this, they suggested, was to tell everyone that a great swathe of the Baltic, where everyone had been merrily fishing for centuries, was actually a solid country. In a stroke of genius, they decided that, since fish have fins, they would name the fake country 'Finland'. Russia, being famously easy-going at the time, happily went along with the idea.

So the two countries, both impoverished by the war, constructed the Trans-Siberian Railway to transfer all that fish, and then Japan went angling. Once the daily quota of sushi ingredients had been caught they would send it via Russia to Japan. Russia took a cut, in the shape of a fraction of the catch, which they fed to their starving population.

While they were about it, they thought they had better change all the world's maps and mariners' charts to make Finland look real. Obviously, the scheme has had to be kept rigorously updated with the latest fake information, on European and American satellite pictures and global positioning systems, without anyone noticing. These days the fish are sent to Japan disguised as 'Nokia' phones.

The people who live in Fake Finland today are really Swedes who don't know it and think they live in a country which is really part of Sweden but looks like what they call Finland. They speak a newly invented Japanese-like language called 'Finnish', one of the most fiendishly difficult in the world, and a whole Finnish cultural, industrial, ethnographic and geological history has been written up, with libraries and museums full of brilliantly forged paintings, historical archives and ancient documents.

Of all the biggest inverted pyramids of piffle, the Fake Finland conspiracy theory is surely the easiest to demolish. Let's look at the historical record.

After the war Japan was truly in a bad way, but America wanted to create a post-war market of customers in the Far East to buy its products. As in West Germany, vast investment quickly turned the country around and the Japanese fishing fleet was soon bigger than it had been before the war. But overfishing didn't raise its head until the sixties, and the Trans-Siberian Railway was already old at the time of the alleged Fake Finland scheme.

'Finland' is an ancient name that appears from at least the eleventh century, and is thought to be related to the tribe name 'Finns'. The meaning of the name is disputed but it has nothing to do with fish.

Finland has been clearly visible from Estonia for ever. If you get on a ferry in Tallinn it will arrive in Helsinki in a couple of hours. On a clear night the lights of the Finnish city are easily seen, though Fake Finland conspiracy theorists maintain that these are from Japanese fishing boats.

This supposed conspiracy is one of those that is just too big to be feasible, and the reason we know for sure that Fake Finland is a fake conspiracy is that a journalist managed to track down the person who, quite by accident, let this hare out of the trap.

Mack Lamoureux, a reporter from *Vice* magazine, wrote up the story in December 2016, in an article headlined 'This Dude Accidentally Convinced the Internet That Finland Doesn't Exist'. Lamoureux identified the fellow who started the whole thing off, but let us call him 'Patient Zero'.

It all began with his oddly worded post on Reddit: *'What did your parents show you to do that you assumed was completely normal, only to later discover that it was not normal at all?'* This was followed by his own answer:

> *My parents never believed in Finland, I grew up to never believe in Finland until I researched it further ... firstly they say that the actual 'place of Finland' is just Eastern Sweden ... World maps are altered as it's a UN conspiracy to keep people believing in Finland ... Finland's main company, Nokia, is apparently owned by the Japanese and they're a main player in this ... It's mostly to do*

with Japanese fishing rights ... There are loads
more that they go on about but I can't remember it
all at the moment.

It all sounds so innocuous, but once the blue touch paper
had been lit there was no stopping the firework display
that followed. If only Patient Zero had slept on it before
posting, we could have been spared so much mental
anguish. Or as the Finns say, '*Aamu on iltaa viisaampi*'
('The morning is wiser than the evening').

'Pizzagate'

Some conspiracy theories are supported by evidence, others have evidence both in their favour and against, and a number are simply false. A few people find sorting out which is which a bit tricky.

No such problem attaches to 'Pizzagate', another thoroughly debunked conspiracy theory that went viral in the run-up to the 2016 US presidential election but which has been discredited by everybody who has looked into it, including the Washington, DC police. So, what exactly was it and why did it go viral?

The title 'Pizzagate' arose from the journalistic dodge of attaching '-gate' to the end of any word you wish to turn into a cause célèbre, giving it the flavour of the Watergate scandal (*see page 165*). It's an old trick: remember 'Irangate', 'Squidgygate' and 'Monicagate'? All of them somehow absorbed authority from the '-gate' suffix.

'Pizzagate' all started in March 2016, when the personal email account of Hillary Clinton's presidential campaign manager John Podesta was hacked and WikiLeaks published his emails. Very quickly conspiracy theorists claimed these contained secret messages, including the highly suspicious codename 'cheese pizza', which appeared to connect prominent Democrat Party wonks with human trafficking and a supposed child sex ring run out of a restaurant.

Just a moment's thought would have tipped off even the most credulous person that this irresponsible and false suggestion was absurdly improbable. Nonetheless the claims took off, as members of the alt-right – a ragbag of 'alternative-right-wing' extreme nationalists and white supremacists – began posting claims on the internet, their natural home. These often anonymous characters, posting on platforms such as 4chan, Reddit, Facebook and Twitter, were soon joined by 'conservative' journalists. In a single month, nearly a million messages were reportedly sent using the term 'Pizzagate'.

One of the restaurants that came under fire was the Comet Ping Pong pizzeria in Washington, DC. The owner of Comet Ping Pong, James Alefantis, happened to be a Democrat Party supporter and his name had appeared in the Podesta emails. After trawling Alefantis's Instagram feed, posters conjured up an imaginary paedophile sex ring involving prominent politicians and political donors, run by Hillary Clinton from the basement of the restaurant. The claims were entirely fake, and not all that clever. 'They ignore basic truths,' said Alefantis. 'We don't even have a basement.'

Alefantis and his staff began receiving death threats. Then, one day in December, a devoutly revved-up Christian named Edgar Maddison Welch decided to 'self-investigate' the 'corrupt system' that, as he put it, 'kidnaps, tortures, and rapes babies and children in our own backyard'. He did this not by researching and cross-checking the information but by travelling from North Carolina to Washington, in faded jeans and a beard, and carrying a horrible-looking rifle. He entered the pizza restaurant, where parents and children sat trying to enjoy a family meal, and fired his gun. Looking for the non-existent basement, he opened a door and found himself in a cupboard. It would have been funny if it hadn't been so dangerous. Very luckily, nobody was hurt. After his arrest he told the *New York Times*, 'The intel on this wasn't a hundred per cent.' Neither, it seems, were his critical faculties. He was sent down for four years.

Comet Ping Pong owner James Alefantis said he considered the incident a 'politically orchestrated attack'. Professor of social psychology at Anglia Ruskin University Viren Swami, who has studied conspiracy beliefs in detail, also believes that in the US, 'conspiracy theorising is being deployed as a political weapon. And that's a very big change in the way that conspiracy narratives are being used.' In the West such theories have typically been favoured by people who lack agency or power. A simplistic conspiracy theory gives them the capacity to challenge government – to ask questions. But more recently, says, Swami, politicians such as sometime US President Donald Trump have used conspiracy theories to mobilise support, by propagating crude fabrications like Pizzagate.

The claim that a paedophile sex ring is being run from the basement of a restaurant with no basement is not only a logical error, it is also something easily checkable by anyone who can reach the restaurant, without the need to fire rifles near the heads of children. But evidence is irrelevant in such political operations. People believe wild theories for different reasons, and some will believe almost anything, especially if it is strongly emotional in content.

In 2016 Swami published research showing that such theories are more likely to be believed by people who are going through stressful experiences. Some may be suffering a mental disorder, but for others such theories provide simple explanations for confusing events, especially events threatening to their self-esteem.

President Donald Trump captured the hearts of many in America's once busy but now crumbling Rust Belt by normalising belief in the most extreme conspiracy theories. The idea that there are simply 'good' people and 'bad' people, and that the president is eager to protect you from the 'bad', provides the spark that ignites the flame of simple belief. In a landscape of disappointment, loss, confusion and fear for the future, such beliefs place believers on the side of the morally righteous and provide simple certainties and a sense of 'belonging'.

But Swami says those who readily believe such wacky conspiracy theories are likely to move from mainstream politics into the politics of the fringe. They are also far more likely, he says, to 'engage with racist, xenophobic and extremist views'. Presenting people with accurate information that demystifies and debunks demonstrably false theories can diminish belief among those who have yet to make up their minds, explains Swami. But hoping to change the minds of those who have already made them up is pretty well doomed to failure.

The Wayfair Conspiracy

In the summer of 2020, weird rumours began circulating on social media that a US-based online furniture and home-goods business named Wayfair was selling 'missing children'. The claims began in June 2020 on QAnon (*see page 199*), a quirky outfit whose underlying thesis when it began was that a secret plot against former President Trump was being run by the 'deep state'. The first poster was concerned about the 'high prices' of furniture labelled with female names. Following up on this, a tweeter using the misspelled hashtag '#Wayfairtrafficing' said: 'They've named these over priced (*sic*) cabinets after missing children … cause they are selling children … this is how the elites do things right in your face.'

These early musings provoked little interest, but about a month later the accusation reappeared on the 'conspiracy' part of the Reddit discussion website. Now, with the Reddit wind behind it, this tiny spark caused the eruption of a full-blown child-trafficking-conspiracy wildfire.

There did seem something odd about those prices. Some of Wayfair's 'utility closets' and desks came in at more than $17,000. That appeared too high for ordinary bits of furniture. But perhaps strangest of all were the female names. To the Wayfair 'true believers', it seemed obvious: the website was cataloguing girls, identifying them by name on very expensive cupboards, and, instead of the ludicrously priced items, sending these children to customers. A Twitter user who found a set of pillows and shower curtains costing $9,999 was angry, and put their point in shouty capitals and mangled syntax: 'Wayfair also supplies the furniture at ICE detention centers where children are going MISSING from.' There was quite a lot of swearing too, but I've left that out.

A bemused Wayfair spokesperson told Reuters that the company used a product-naming algorithm, which applied 'first names, geographic locations, and common words for naming purposes'. They told *USA Today*: 'The products in question are industrial grade cabinets that are accurately priced,' although, as it appeared, there had also been a computer glitch with some of the $9.99-type prices, which had been inflated to ludicrous amounts by the accidental addition of extra nines – a not uncommon fault.

Wayfair briefly removed some products from their site to rename them, and, they said, 'to provide a more in-depth description and photos that accurately depict the product to clarify the price point'. But this wordy business-speak only increased suspicion among the conspiracy buffs, and as the false rumours swirled around the globe Wayfair found itself obliged to respond with an official denial: 'There is of course no truth to these claims,' they said tersely – possibly making twirly finger-circles beside their heads as they said it. All the same, though inherently improbable – it would surely take a very big pillow to contain a child – there was something especially intriguing about this particular conspiracy theory, and reports rapidly began to appear in the mainstream press around the world. According to data from Facebook's CrowdTangle analytics, the term 'Wayfair' generated four million engagements on Instagram from all over the world. BBC Monitoring reported vast (unexplained) interest in Turkey – the country, not the poultry.

The viral spread continued via so-called 'social media influencers', who now distributed increasingly rich and detailed allegations among their followers. By sharing the conspiracy theory online, Maddie Thompson, who described herself as 'a microblading artist, creator, entrepreneur, and social media maven', more than doubled her Instagram following to 44,000. Her husband Justin Thompson, who wears his baseball hat back to front, recorded himself ordering a $17,337.98 Wayfair desk to prove the theory, though in the end Wayfair did not send him a child instead of the furniture.

Next, QAnon followers tried to link the female first names of the Wayfair furniture to particular missing children. For example, the 'Samiyah 5 – self-storage cabinet' ($12,899.99) was said to contain seventeen-year-old Samiyah Mumin, who, according to records, went missing in Ohio in 2019. However, in July 2020 a woman who said she was Samiyah Mumin explained on Facebook Live that, actually, she wasn't missing.

But QAnon activists are nothing if not dogged, and some began putting stock-keeping numbers of Wayfair products into Russian search engine Yandex. What happened was that their searches returned pictures of young women. When *Newsweek* explored the process, using an old-fashioned journalistic technique called 'checking your facts', they found that any random string of numbers would produce the same results.

There are many lessons to learn from the Wayfair fiasco about the way online conspiracy theories begin, grow and spread globally on social media. They often begin with one person's unsupported suggestion, which may be a confusion, or a joke, and occasionally a deliberate untruth. If unchecked, they feed on themselves and grow extra heads, until they resemble the Hydra. A good way to permanently chop off some of those heads is to start by saying to yourself: 'What if everything I believe about everything is possibly wrong?' This is a great drain cleaner for the mind, though it may do little to persuade true believers, for whom doubt is a slippery slope that undermines the core of their thinking style and is hard to recover from. Even reasoned argument, supported by evidence from a variety of reliable sources, is likely to bounce off these folks, like a dried pea dropped on a kettledrum. All the same, it's worth a try.

Sometimes a conspiracy theory has entirely undesirable effects. In the case of Wayfair unintended harmful consequences were revealed in a press release from the US National Human Trafficking Hotline, which said they had received so many calls based on the Wayfair conspiracy theory that it made it 'more difficult … to provide support and attention to others who are in need of help'.

The bald truth is that the strangely compelling Wayfair 'child-trafficking' business was based entirely on one person's unease about some expensive furniture, an unjustified and unholy leap of speculation, and wild viral spread by some people who forgot to check their facts. In the end, no evidence was offered to give any credence whatever to this conspiracy theory, though whether it will last or fade away remains to be seen.

#FreeBritney

In the old days it was newspaper articles and gossip that gave life to new conspiracy theories, but with the explosion of social media in recent years, they spread like grape rot. Then, as now, some stuck while others withered on the vine.

Many of the most popular conspiracy theories involve internationally important or famous people. Whether they are politicians such as Presidents Kennedy or Trump, or pop superstars such as Elvis Presley or Paul McCartney, only narcissists, and personalities of the greatest mental stoutness, can manage the constant scrutiny and endless paparazzi-probing that goes with fame. Rich and successful though they may be, some performers, especially the young, do not have the psychological reserves to deal with the endless critical attention, which would frazzle the emotional wellbeing of anybody normal. This seems to have been what happened to the multi-millionaire pop superstar Britney Spears.

Spears signed up with Jive Records in 1997 at the age of just fifteen, becoming the bestselling teenage artist of all time. She has been phenomenally successful around the world: her first two studio albums, ... *Baby One*

More Time (1999) and *Oops! … I Did It Again* (2000), are two of the biggest albums ever, and newspapers dubbed her the 'Princess of Pop'. Britney has a huge following on social media and YouTube, including channels 'BritneySpears BS' and plain old 'Britney Spears' – which has many millions of subscribers.

Professional success is one thing, psychological well-being another, and the singer's emotional health has featured in the news for many years. Her erratic behaviour was first reported in 2007 following her divorce and the loss of custody of her two children, after she refused to give up her sons in a deadlock with police. Other press stories of the singer's 'mental breakdown' have included tales of her shaving her head, and hitting a photographer's car with an umbrella. In April 2020 she reportedly told followers that she had accidentally burned down her home gym. Whether suffering a fire in your house, cutting your hair and hitting an annoying photographer's car with an umbrella are mental problems – or just life happening – is a question some journalists might like to ask themselves.

In any case, a so-called 'conservatorship' was put in place in 2008 and Britney found herself in psychiatric care. A US court grants a conservatorship when a person – for example, a dementia patient – cannot make his or her own decisions. The terms of Spears's conservatorship allowed her father, Jamie Spears, along with a lawyer, to control her visitors and to speak to doctors about her treatment.

During the decade or so that her life has been governed by the conservatorship, Britney Spears has produced three albums, appeared time after time on television and held a Las Vegas residency. But in January 2019 she announced she would be stopping work for a while after her father nearly died from a colonic rupture. Shortly afterwards she entered a 'psychiatric facility'.

In a November 2020 court case, Britney's lawyer said the pop star was 'afraid' of her father, had no 'viable working relationship' with him and that the pair had not spoken in a 'long while'. Her mother called their relationship 'toxic'. According to US news website TMZ, her lawyers had already submitted papers saying she was 'strongly opposed' to her father's continuing control, and had filed documents opposing his motion to keep facts 'hidden away in the closet as a family secret', as they put it. Though the court rejected Spears's attempt to have her father removed as conservator, a judge said future appeals would be considered.

A podcast entitled *Britney's Gram* claimed that Spears's father was, in fact, keeping her against her will, which led to fifty or so of Britney's fans assembling outside West Hollywood City Hall wielding posters with the hashtag #FreeBritney. This online movement was born in 2009, the year after the conservatorship was announced, but the latest developments had given it new life. Waving a petition of more than 125,000 signatures, campaigners explained to the media that they had asked the White House to end the conservatorship, gaining the support of glamorous celebrities Cher, Paris Hilton and Miley Cyrus, as well as the unglamorous but influential American Civil Liberties Union.

In fact, Spears's dad had already tried to close down #FreeBritney, and, in his own quirky, ungrammatical style, had this to say about its members: 'All these conspiracy theorists don't know anything … The world don't have a clue. It's up to the court of California to decide what's best for my daughter. It's no one else's business.'

The court, however, had other ideas, announcing that, 'Far from being a conspiracy theory or a "joke", as James [Jamie] reportedly told the media, in large part this scrutiny is a reasonable and even predictable result of James's aggressive use of the sealing procedure over the years to minimize the amount of meaningful information made available to the public.'

The funny thing is, though, that some of the lurid claims Britney's fans were making do look very much like conspiracy theories. For example, in 2020, supporters suggested that her carers were putting out old videos to give the false impression that she was okay. Some who said she had been pleading for help on social media told her that, if she was in need of help, she should post a painting of doves, or a photograph of herself in a yellow shirt. Quite why they chose these things is a mystery; it's not as if everyone keeps a painting of doves knocking about somewhere just in case.

Perhaps trying to calm the fervour, Spears did, in fact, share a date-stamped picture of herself, encouraging fans to 'check the date'. But to the ardent conspiracists this was exactly the proof of their claim they had been waiting for. 'The fact you need to post the date to prove she's real,' said one, 'looks really suspicious … we all know someone's running the account.'

A person's psychological wellbeing is surely a private matter. The prurient preoccupation with the personal emotional lives of the rich and famous that you see all over social media cannot help those people. A compulsory part of fame should not be the examination of your every look and utterance. For someone with a history of psychiatric troubles it cannot be helpful to have followers calling your existence into question. Aren't the conspiracy theories of fans that result in instructions to wear certain clothes, or to confirm your identity, as unwelcome as the oppressive rules of a conservatorship or the demands of an overbearing father?

Whether Jamie Spears was correct in his characterisation of the #FreeBritney people as a bunch of conspiracy theorists depends on your point of view. Though he sounds a bit of a rough diamond, and though he has an unusual relationship with his daughter, maybe he was right in his assessment of the #FreeBritney community as conspiracy mongers.

Those unlikely bedfellows the American Civil Liberties Union and Paris Hilton have come to the opposite conclusion. Having carefully considered all the #FreeBritney evidence, they see the whole BS conspiracy-theory accusation as pure BS.

Denver International Airport

As you drive in to Denver International Airport the first intimations that something strange is going on is a sculpture of a thirty-two-foot-tall blue mustang (known as Blucifer) with lit-up red eyes. This horse has been seen as cursed ever since a bit fell off and killed its sculptor. Some say it is modelled on the pale horse of the Apocalypse, from the Book of Revelation, yet what I noticed was its alarmingly detailed nether regions, covered in weird veins.

Opened in 1995, Denver International Airport (DIA) is the second largest airport in the world. From its earliest days, conspiracy theories have swirled around its runways like a flock of starlings, variously proposing that it is a new secret headquarters for the Illuminati (*see page 187*), Neo-Nazis, Lizard Men (*see page 192*) or the New World Order (*see page 149*). Others suggest it was built to conceal huge underground bunkers to be used as a home for aliens during the forthcoming apocalypse, a concentration camp for US citizens or a fallout shelter for the world's elite. In 2010, a claim emerged that this apocalypse would happen in 2012, but, 2012 having come and gone, that theory is not much discussed any more. The caverns are indeed vast and include two tunnels, each about twenty football pitches long. It is said that when airport officials are questioned about these mysterious chambers, they say they are not allowed to discuss it.

All these theories rest on DIA's many distinctive design features, from masonic symbols cut into the airport's dedication stone, to the shape of the runways, which are said, from the air, to resemble a 'Nazi swastika'.

The new Denver International Airport replaced the old Stapleton International airport, built in 1929, which had six runways, while the new DIA has only five. This seemed extremely suspicious. Why spend all this money on a new airport with fewer runways and vast, empty underground bunkers? And why would an airport need a fuelling system that can pump 1,000 gallons of fuel per minute, an amount described as 'totally absurd for a commercial airport'. What was going on?

When I looked into these questions some interesting facts emerged. First: the problem of a redundant new airport replacing a perfectly good one with more runways. It turns out that, because of the airport's design, only three of Stapleton's six runways could be used at any one time and it was frantically overcrowded, with continual delays. DIA's five runways can be used simultaneously and support the largest jets, getting around the delay problem. Furthermore, being just five miles from Denver city centre, Stapleton had been repeatedly sued for noise nuisance. The replacement Denver International is twenty-five miles out, and has had no noise complaints.

Contrary to the allegation that airport officials refuse to discuss the underground space, they actually do tours of the tunnels, which were initially built to house the new airport's much-heralded automated luggage-management system. In time-honoured airport-design style, this never worked and was a total money-losing disaster. Today the tunnels are used for baggage handling in the old-fashioned way. I also read an assessment of the fuelling-system business by Gary Austerman, a senior airport fuelling-systems planner, and learnt that a fill rate of 1,000 gallons per minute is not 'totally absurd', as it has been called, but quite normal for modern aircraft in an airport of this kind.

While I was about it, I had a quick look at an aerial shot of the 'Nazi-design' runways. Only when I squinted hard did these look anything like a swastika, and then only vaguely. Then there was that business with the 'dedication capstone' with sinister masonic markings. I found a picture of the stone, which indeed contains several masonic references, including a huge masonic square and compasses. The only thing that struck me about this stone, though, was the truly amateurish letter-cutting. The abysmally engraved, ill-spaced capitals make it almost illegible. How ironic for Masons, whose business this surely is. They should also know that a capstone is normally fixed on top of something. This great big lump of granite is on the *floor*, where it looks like a shocking trip hazard.

Carved on this ugly lump are the words 'New World Airport Commission'. 'New World Airport' looks similar to 'New World Order', and conspiracy 'researchers' say it is 'a blatant sign' that the airport is under the control of the Freemasons and the New World Order. A tired airport spokesman explained that the New World Airport Commission was a just group of local politicians and businesspeople, presumably including the local masonic lodges, who had drummed up a bit of money for the airport's construction.

The stone bears the date 19 March 1994 (191994). Theorists say that if you add these numbers – 1, 9, 1, 9, 9 and 4 – you get 33, which is apparently the highest degree in Masonry. But, hang on, there are other ways to express that date. If you include the month (03) you get the series 19031994. Add that lot up and you get 36: the age of death of both Marilyn Monroe and Princess Diana. Wow! What's more, if you divide the series at its midpoint you get 1903–1994, which are the birth and death dates of my great-aunt Maureen, who lived near Blubberhouses, near Harrogate, in the seventies. How incredible is that?! Anyway, if the Masons are trying to keep their involvement a big secret, why are they boasting about it on their stone?

Creepily engraved here and there throughout the airport are the periodic table symbols for gold and silver, *Au* and *Ag*, said to reflect Denver's mining history. It has been claimed, though, that a deadly new strain of hepatitis B produces a toxin known as 'Australia Antigen', which has *Au Ag* as its abbreviation, and that this virus will be used by the New World Order, or one of the other usual suspects, to reduce the population when

Armageddon strikes. When I looked up this Australia Antigen virus, I found that it's actually known as 'HBsAg', which is not engraved anywhere in the airport. If you just check a few things, it's amazing what you can discover.

Looking up from the *Au* and *Ag* inscriptions we find several huge multi-coloured murals perpetrated by someone called Leo Tanguma. These have become infamous for their weird imagery, showing sentimentalised children of all races, national flags and what has been called a 'Nazi', or sometimes 'Russian', stormtrooper with a scimitar, 'violently molesting' a dove's backside. Other subjects liable to make your airport lunch come back up at you appear on other murals, which together have been described as 'a New World Order manifesto' that depicts the aims of massive depopulation and one world government. A mural entitled 'Children of the World Dream of Peace' has been described by a certain conspiracy theorist as showing 'America joyfully submitting to Germany', with children eagerly giving weapons to a 'German boy' who is holding a hammer 'and apparently building something'. What the painting actually shows is a boy of indeterminate nationality being handed swords, which he is hammering into ploughshares, the famous metaphor from Isaiah 2:4, and one of the Bible's finest messages: 'And they shall beat their swords into ploughshares, and their spears into pruninghooks: nation shall not lift up sword against nation, neither shall they learn war any more.' All this seems to have escaped our conspiracy expert. Anyway, Mr Tanguma denies the theories of his paintings' New World Order meanings, saying his murals actually represent peace and hope.

In 2018 'Children of the World Dream of Peace' was painted over, setting off more conspiracy theories, though it may just have been that airport officials were heartily sick of their days being spoilt by these amateurish daubs, which are the sort of vulgar enormities Saddam Hussein would have had on his wall, next to his gold toilet. Who knows, perhaps they were even sponsored by airline sick-bag manufacturers?

The Pizza-slice Plot

Shane Dawson, a YouTuber in his thirties, jumped onto the video platform in 2005, and in a twinkling had become one of its biggest stars, posting videos in which he and his friends consider the most pressing conspiracy theories of our time.

One of Shane's best conspiracy investigations is to be seen in his YouTube video, cleverly entitled 'Investigating Conspiracies with Shane Dawson'. It occurs about twenty-one minutes into the one-and-a-half-hour film and is an exhaustive probe into a well-established conspiracy theory about the pizzas from 'eatertainment' restaurant chain Chuck E. Cheese, the slices of which sometimes do not align correctly. What could be the sinister reasons behind this aberration?

Dawson's video is classified on YouTube as a comedy, though it includes the grim story of a woman who narrowly avoided human trafficking. Whatever the case, it was the pizza-slice business that caught everyone's eye: what in the name of all that's holy was going on with these pizzas, and who was responsible?

Dawson explained it this way: 'So I noticed this when I was eight years old or something. I was like, "Wait a minute, how come all the pieces are different?"' It must have been just like Isaac Newton wondering why the apple was falling downwards, and the theory of gravity coming to him in a flash.

In his video, Dawson visits a Chuck E. Cheese place, where he orders a couple of pizzas and, sure enough, both seem to have slices that just don't match up. Dawson was blunt in his reaction to this creepy anomaly: 'I mean, that's undeniable, that's crazy,' he said.

It was time for me to look into things, and doing my own research I found photos on TripAdvisor that exposed the chilling truth: the crusts and cuts on more than just some of Chuck E. Cheese's pizza slices plainly fail to line up exactly with each other, in extreme cases causing slivers of pepperoni to form disturbingly misaligned semicircles at the slice junctions. Was the carefully hidden reason behind this anomalous alignment that the company was recycling left-behind pizza segments in newly assembled Frankenstein pizzas?

Well, before you could read 'Sodium acid pyrophosphate' off the ingredients list on the side of a pizza box, the peculiar-pizza video had notched up many millions of views. By the time viewers were up to the pizza-slice section, most had probably already forgotten the unobtrusively displayed 'for entertainment purposes only' disclaimer explaining that Shane Dawson's exhaustive investigation of this deeply troubling mystery of the century was 'just a theory' and not a statement of fact. 'Disclaimer' is a technical term better known to non-specialists as 'arse covering', but it comes in handy nonetheless.

Many of Dawson's YouTube fans seemed to agree with his careful scientific analysis of this important strange-ness of pizza-slice alignment, but, as usual, moany sceptical voices soon piped up. Among them were members of the restaurant's staff, who, wiping the flour off their hands, got onto their phones to offer their expert Occam's-razor-type explanations. One explained that when the pizzas are transferred to the 'pizza platter' from the surface on which they have been cut, the slices move about, disrupting the immaculate circumference and the perfect internal mosaic of pizza toppings. Especially, she said, when they put a large pizza into an 'Xlarge pizza platter'. Another said: 'It's people in the kitchen just not giving a crap.'

The faceless parent company of Chuck E. Cheese is CEC Entertainment, Inc., which is a typically chilling Big Hospitality name. Their anonymous press people moving about in the shadows put out a couple of predictable, no doubt deliberately boring, corporate responses. 'The claims made in this video about Chuck E. Cheese's and our pizza are unequivocally false,' they said without a smile. And: 'We prep the dough daily for our made-to-order pizzas, which means they're not always perfectly round, but they are still great tasting.'

All the same, in May 2020 the *New York Post* reported that Chuck E. Cheese was now doing business on food delivery apps, under a completely redesigned logo, as Pasqually's Pizza & Wings. Was there something sinister in this, or is this conspiracy theory another of those moonshine ones? Whatever Shane Dawson says, he does have his critics, who obsess over 'quality', while making no allowance for the huge numbers of fans who endlessly watch his videos. Twenty-three million subscribers and more than five billion viewers can't be wrong. Can they?

While we're on the subject it seems to me there is a conspiracy going on with all the calories, and all the fat, not to mention all the salt, you get in pizzas. I have to drink about five pints of water after dining off a big one. In fact, I just looked up a typical pizza and found it contains 376 per cent of your recommended daily sodium allowance – nearly four days' worth of salt – and 3,753 calories, 42 per cent of which is fat. Even if you have only a couple of skinny slices, you'll have blown 624 calories. Are Big Pizza trying to make us all so obese that we become addicted to their products? *There's* a conspiracy really worth looking into.

The Dihydrogen Monoxide Conspiracy

An analysis of the world's wildest conspiracy theories would be nothing without an investigation into what must be the most sinister and best-kept government conspiracy since the days of the Knights Templar (*see page 80*).

Thanks largely to the sterling work of conspiracy theorist and éminence grise Tom Way, and his campaigning organisation DHMO.org, we now know a great deal about the worldwide conspiracy that is the dihydrogen monoxide scandal.

Dihydrogen monoxide is a deadly chemical compound used in everything from spray-on oven cleaners to nuclear reactors. It is an industrial reactant that works as a powerful fire-retardant, and a solvent so corrosive it eats holes into solid metal. It can mutate DNA, disrupt cell membranes and chemically alter vital neurotransmitters; should you get even a small amount in your eye it can cause acute palpebral nictitation. Ingestion of this highly reactive hydroxyl radical can produce abdominal distension and diuresis, while accidental inhalation results in many deaths each year in every inhabited country of the world.

Like hydrogen sulfide, dihydrogen monoxide is a hydrogen chalcogenide. It has no detectible smell and is colourless, so its presence easily goes unnoticed. It may shock you to learn that there is already a significant amount of this heavy compound in your body.

Its frequent use in cosmetic products is often concealed by the cynical adoption of alternative names. The terms dihydrogen oxide, hydrogen hydroxide, oxidane and hydric acid may be used when the true identity of DHMO is being deliberately concealed from the public. It has been detected in varying amounts in household cleaning products, shampoo and shower gel, children's ice cream, hospital beverages and even in baby food.

DHMO is used in industrial quantities for its so-called 'moistening' action in high-fat cakes and pies, and has been found too in the most popular brands of high-sugar, high-calorie soft drinks. It is commonly artificially added to soil by the developers of genetically modified crops.

Owing to deliberately lax legal requirements, factories and sewage works are free to pump very large quantities of this corrosive acid into rivers and public waterways. The coastal areas around Scotland contain very large amounts of dihydrogen monoxide, as do the crabbing grounds off the Norfolk coast, and the organisation Surfers Against Sewage says 'detectable amounts' have been found attached to surfboards and wetsuits after even brief exposure. Its presence has been recorded on the peak of Mount Everest and in the depths of the Marianas Trench, 35,853 feet below the surface of the Western Pacific Ocean.

THE DIHYDROGEN MONOXIDE CONSPIRACY

The liquid, solid and gaseous forms of DHMO are all major contributory factors in many serious air crashes, and in its gaseous form it causes severe burns, especially to children. Lengthy exposure to its rarer solid type leads to nerve and blood vessel destruction, tissue necrosis and limb amputation.

Dihydrogen monoxide has been found in large amounts in public swimming pools, where pool operators claim it 'maintains chemical balance'. Although it results in deaths every year in pools, its use is not illegal.

While well aware of the dangers of dihydrogen monoxide, the UK government – as is true of governments worldwide – does not classify it as toxic or cancer causing, as it does with other dangerous compounds. Though communist North Korea, China and Russia together exceed the amounts used by even the USA, its use is practically never referred to, and even the parliaments of democratic countries fail to treat it as controversial, maybe because they have all adopted it extensively themselves. It is, perhaps, no surprise that these governments are well aware of the inconvenient truth that if its use were forbidden industry would grind to a halt.

Though most people have never heard of DHMO, overwhelming numbers, when surveyed and told of its harmful effects, believe it should be banned. One researcher said that if only people paid closer attention to the available information about dihydrogen monoxide more of them would know the truth, and the time-consuming public information efforts of the kind done, for example, by DHMO.org would be unnecessary.

Here is a short list of some of the other dangers of dihydrogen monoxide:

- Exposure to DHMO decreases the effectiveness of vehicle brakes and is the direct cause of many road accidents every year in the UK and abroad.
- Dihydrogen monoxide is deliberately added to the food given to banned pit bull terriers and other dangerous dogs.
- It is consciously given to soldiers worldwide to improve their performance in the field. Vast amounts were dispensed to servicemen, much of it in their food, during the Iraq War, ostensibly to 'keep them going'.
- It has been used to greatly heighten the effect of so-called 'waterboarding'.

Pressure groups, such as DHMO.org, which fight to encourage the public to think carefully about this compound and its deliberately confusing names, have had very little success combatting this conspiracy, which has been called the most closely guarded secret of the military–industrial complex. Why is something so harmful, corrosive and dangerous to humans almost universally used by faceless industry without governments objecting? Can it just be the economic benefits or is there a more sinister purpose behind it? What is one to believe?

Well, the only reason to believe this, or any, conspiracy theory would be that it was probably true. To find out the probability of something in nature being true you must examine the evidence. This is the only way. If the evidence doesn't agree with the conspiracy theory, then the theory is *false*.

For example, if you check every statement I've made above, you will find not only that it's true, but that it seems to point squarely in a particular direction. If, though, you shift your point of view a little, you will find it pointing in an equally uncompromising manner to something entirely different.

So, hold onto your hat: dihydrogen monoxide is just another name for water (H_2O), which has two hydrogen molecules (dihydrogen) and one oxygen molecule (monoxide). Yes, it can be dangerous but without it we'd all be dead. The director of DHMO.org is Dr Tom Way, Associate Professor of Computer Science at Villanova University, in Pennsylvania. His satirical website is designed to encourage people to add an appropriate dollop of scepticism to scientific-sounding scare stories, and to get people to think twice before swallowing bucket-loads of unnerving facts. Some conspiracy theories will be true, some will have a bit of truth in them and some will be pure mumbo jumbo. To steer a safe course between the true and the false it is vital to cultivate the art of doubt, especially concerning your own biases, convictions and certainties. But go careful! It's good to keep an open mind, but not so open that your brains fall out.